A FALCON FIELD GUIDE ™

Birds of Texas

Todd Telander

FALCONGUIDES

GUILFORD, CONNECTICUT
HELENA, MONTANA

AN IMPRINT OF GLOBE PEQUOT PRESS

To my wife, Kirsten, my children, Miles and Oliver, and my parents, all of whom have supported and encouraged me through the years. Special thanks to Mike Denny for his expert critique of the illustrations.

To buy books in quantity for corporate use or incentives, call **(800) 962-0973** or e-mail **premiums@GlobePequot.com**.

FALCONGUIDES ®

MIX
Paper from responsible sources
FSC® C005010
www.fsc.org

FalconGuides is an imprint of Globe Pequot Press.
Falcon Field Guides is a trademark and Falcon, FalconGuides, and Outfit Your Mind are registered trademarks of Morris Book Publishing, LLC.

Project editor: David Legere
Text design: Sheryl P. Kober
Layout: Sue Murray

Library of Congress Cataloging-in-Publication Data is available on file.

ISBN 978-0-7627-7420-3

Printed in the United States of America

10 9 8 7 6 5 4 3 2

Contents

Nonpasserines

Passerines

Introduction

Texas, the largest state in the Lower 48, consists of a great variety of habitats: the coastal plains and Piney Woods forests near the Gulf of Mexico to the east, tropical brush to the south, dry desert to the west, and high plains to the north. This geographic diversity, with its accompanying array of climatic and vegetative zones, provides for an incredible number and variety of bird species. Texas supports habitat for resident breeders and seasonal visitors, as well as those birds passing through on migration to and from South America and Canada. Although Texas is home to or visited by over 600 species of birds, this guide describes the birds you are most likely to encounter here and includes some that are not found anywhere else in the United States, like the Golden-cheeked Warbler and the Great Kiskadee.

Notes about the Species Accounts

Order
The order of species listed in this guide is based on the most recent version of the *Check-List of North American Birds,* published by the American Ornithologists' Union. The arrangement of some groups, especially within the nonpasserines, may be slightly different than that of older field guides but reflects the most recent accepted arrangement.

Names
Both the common name and the scientific name are included for each entry. Since common names tend to vary regionally, or there may be more than one common name for each species, the universally accepted scientific name of genus and species (such as *Pyrocephalus rubinus,* for the Vermillion Flycatcher) is more reliable to be certain of identification. Also, one can often learn interesting facts about a bird by the English translation of its Latin name. For instance, the generic name, *Pyrocephalus,* derives from the latin *pyro,* meaning fire, and *cephalus,* meaning head, describing the fire-red plumage on the head of this flycatcher.

Families
Birds are grouped into families based on similar traits, behaviors, and genetics. When trying to identify an unfamiliar bird, it can often be helpful to first place it into a family, which will reduce your search to a smaller group. For example, if you see a long-legged, long-billed bird lurking in the shallows, you can begin by looking in the family group of Ardeidae (Herons, Egrets), and narrow your search from there.

Size
The size given for each bird is the average length from the tip of the bill to the end of the tail if the bird was laid out flat. Sometimes females and males vary in size, and this variation is described in the

text. Size can be misleading if you are looking at a small bird that happens to have a very long tail or bill. It can be more effective to judge the bird's relative size by comparing the size difference between two or more species.

Season

The season given in the accounts is the time when the greatest number of individuals occur in Texas. Some species are year-round residents that breed here. Others may spend only summers or winters here, and some may be transient, only stopping during the spring or fall migration. Even if only part of the year is indicated for a species, be aware that there may be individuals that arrive earlier or remain for longer than the given time frame. Plumage also changes with the season for many birds, and this is indicated in the text and illustrations.

Habitat

A bird's habitat is one of the first clues to its identification. Note the environment where you see a bird and compare it with the description listed. This can be especially helpful when identifying a bird that shares traits with related species. For example, Bonaparte's Gulls and Laughing Gulls are similar, but Bonaparte's Gulls may be found far inland while Laughing Gulls are strictly coastal.

Illustrations

The illustrations show the adult bird in the plumage most likely to be encountered during the season(s) it is in Texas. If it is likely that you will find more than one type of plumage during this time, the alternate plumage is also shown. For birds that are sexually dimorphic (females and males look different), illustrations of both sexes are usually included. Other plumages, such as those of juveniles and alternate morphs, are described in the text.

Bird Topography and Terms

Bird topography describes the outer surface of a bird and how various anatomical structures fit together. Below is a diagram outlining the terms most commonly used to describe the feathers and bare parts of a bird.

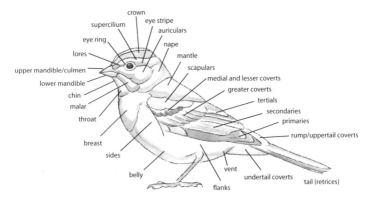

NONPASSERINES

Black-bellied Whistling Duck,
Dendrocygna autumnalis
Family Anatidae (Ducks, Geese)
Size: 21"
Season: Year-round resident in southeast Texas
Habitat: Shallow lakes, ponds, and marshes with nearby trees

The Black-bellied Whistling Duck is a medium-size duck with a flat head and a very long neck and legs, making it appear like a small goose. The back, lower neck, and breast are rusty brown with a black belly, tail, and undertail coverts. The head and upper neck are gray with a dark brown stripe along the crown and nape. The bill is large and orange, and the eyes have white eye-rings. The wings are rounded with a long white stripe, and it holds the head and legs low in flight. Black-bellied Whistling Ducks often feed at night for small invertebrates or plants from marshy fields and ponds. The voice is a series of high, whistled, squeaky notes. It is also known as the "tree duck" due to its habit of roosting and nesting in trees. An adult is illustrated.

Snow Goose, *Chen caerulescens*
Family Anatidae (Ducks, Geese)
Size: 28"
Season: Winter
Habitat: Grasslands, marshes

The Snow Goose forms huge, impressive flocks when it visits Texas during spring and fall migrations between the arctic tundra and southern North America and Mexico, or as it winters here. It has two color forms: the "blue" and the more common "white." The white form is predominantly white, with black outer wing feathers and a pale yellowish wash to the face during summer. The blue form retains the white head and lower belly but is otherwise dark slate gray or brownish-gray. In both morphs, its bill is pink, thick at the base, and has a black patch where the mandibles meet. The legs of both types are pink. Snow Geese feed mostly on the ground, eating shoots, roots, grains, and insects. The similar Ross's Goose is smaller and has a shorter bill. The white morph adult is illustrated.

Wood Duck, *Aix sponsa*
Family Anatidae (Ducks, Geese)
Size: 18"
Season: Year-round
Habitat: Wooded ponds, swamps

The regal Wood Duck is among the dabbling ducks, or those that tip headfirst into shallow water to pluck aquatic plants and animals from the bottom. The male is long tailed and small billed, with a dark back, light buff flanks, and sharp black-and-white head patterning. It also sports a bushy head crest that droops behind the nape. The female is gray-brown with spotting along the underside and a conspicuous white teardrop-shaped eye patch. Both sexes swim with their heads angled downward as if in a nod and have sharp claws, which they use to cling to branches and snags. The breeding female (top) and breeding male (bottom) are illustrated.

Gadwall, *Anas strepera*
Family Anatidae (Ducks, Geese)
Size: 20.5"
Season: Winter
Habitat: Shallow lakes, marshes

The Gadwall is a buoyant, plain-colored dabbling duck with a steep forehead and a somewhat angular head. The breeding male is grayish overall, with very fine variegation and barring. The rump and undertail coverts are black, the scapulars are light orange-brown, the tertials are gray, and the head is lighter below the eye and darker above. Females and nonbreeding males are mottled brownish, with few distinguishing markings. In flight, there is a distinctive white speculum that is most prominent in males. Gadwalls dabble or dive for a variety of aquatic plants and invertebrates, and often gather in large flocks away from the shore. The breeding female (top) and breeding male (bottom) are illustrated.

DUCKS, GEESE

American Widgeon,

Anas americana
Family Anatidae (Ducks, Geese)
Size: 19"
Season: Winter
Habitat: Shallow ponds, fields

The American Widgeon is also known as the Baldpate, in reference to its white crown. A wary and easily alarmed duck, it feeds on the water's surface, often gleaning prey stirred up by the efforts of diving ducks. The underside is a light cinnamon color with white undertail coverts, and the back is light brown. The male has a white crown and forehead with a very slight crest when seen in profile, and a glossy dark green patch extending from the eyes to the back of the neck. A white wing covert patch can usually be seen on the folded wing but is more obvious in flight. The head of the female is unmarked and brownish. The breeding female (top) and breeding male (bottom) are illustrated.

Mallard, *Anas platyrhynchos*

Family Anatidae (Ducks, Geese)
Size: 23"
Season: Year-round
Habitat: Virtually any water environment, parks, urban areas

The ubiquitous Mallard is the most abundant duck in the Northern Hemisphere. It is a classic dabbling duck, plunging its head into the water with its tail up, searching for aquatic plants, animals, and snails, although it will also eat worms, seeds, insects, and even mice. Noisy and quacking, it is heavy but is a strong flier. The male has a dark head with green or blue iridescence, a white neck ring, and a large yellow bill. The underparts are pale, with a chestnut-brown breast. The female is plain brownish, with buff scalloped markings, and has dark eye-lines and an orangey bill with a dark center. The speculum is blue on both sexes, and the tail coverts often curl upward. Mallards form huge floating flocks called "rafts." To achieve flight, it lifts straight into the air without running. The breeding female (top) and breeding male (bottom) are illustrated.

Blue-winged Teal, *Anas discors*

Family Anatidae (Ducks, Geese)
Size: 16"
Season: Winter in southeastern Texas, summer in northern Texas
Habitat: Freshwater marshes and mudflats, wet agricultural areas

The Blue-winged Teal, also known as the White-faced Teal, is a small duck that skims the water surface for aquatic plants and invertebrates, often forming large flocks. The male is mottled brown below, with a prominent white patch near the hip area, and is dark above, with gray on the head and a white vertical crescent at the base of the bill. The female is brownish, with scalloped flanks and a plain head with dark eye-lines, and is pale at the lores. Both sexes have a light blue wing patch visible in flight. The breeding female (top) and breeding male (bottom) are illustrated.

Northern Shoveler,
Anas clypeata
Family Anatidae (Ducks, Geese)
Size: 19"
Season: Winter
Habitat: Shallow marshes, lakes, bays

Also known as the Spoonbill Duck, the Northern Shoveler skims the surface of the water with its neck extended, scooping up aquatic animals and plants with its long, spatulate bill. It will also suck up the ooze from mud and strain it through bristles at the edge of its bill, retaining worms, leeches, and snails. This medium-size duck seems top-heavy due to its large bill. Plumage in the male is white beneath, with a large chestnut side patch, and it has a dark green head and gray bill. The female is pale brownish overall, with an orangey bill. The breeding female (top) and breeding male (bottom) are illustrated.

Northern Pintail, *Anas acuta*
Family Anatidae (Ducks, Geese)
Size: 21"
Season: Winter
Habitat: Marshes, shallow lakes, coastal bays

Among the most abundant ducks in North America, the Northern Pintail is an elegant, slender dabbling duck with a long neck, small head, and narrow wings. In breeding plumage, the male has long, pointed central tail feathers. It is gray along the back and sides, with a brown head and a white breast. A white stripe extends from the breast along the back of the neck. The female is mottled brown and tan overall, with a light brown head. To feed, the Northern Pintail bobs its head into the water to capture aquatic invertebrates and plants from the muddy bottom. It rises directly out of the water to take flight. The breeding female (top) and breeding male (bottom) are illustrated.

Green-winged Teal,
Anas crecca
Family Anatidae (Ducks, Geese)
Size: 14"
Season: Winter
Habitat: Marshes, ponds

The Green-winged Teal is a cute, very small, active duck with a small, thin bill. The breeding male is silvery gray, with a dotted tawny breast patch, a pale yellow hip patch, and a distinct vertical white bar on its side. The head is rusty brown, with an iridescent green patch around and behind the eye. Females and nonbreeding males are mottled brown with dark eye-lines and white belly. Green-winged Teals dabble in the shallows for plant material and small invertebrates. They are quick and agile in flight, and sport a bright green speculum. They form very large winter flocks. The breeding female (top) and breeding male (bottom) are illustrated.

Redhead, *Aythya americana*
Family Anatidae (Ducks, Geese)
Size: 19"
Season: Winter
Habitat: Shallow lakes, marshes

The Redhead is a heavy-bodied diving duck with a steep forehead and a large, rounded head. The breeding male is pale gray, with a dark rear end and breast. The head is light rusty brown, the eyes are yellow, and the bill is bluish with a black tip. The female is brownish-gray overall, with pale areas at the base of the bill and throat. In both sexes, the upper side of the wing has white flight feathers and dark gray coverts. These birds "run" across the water to become airborne. They forage by diving for aquatic plants and invertebrates, and may form huge floating "rafts" during the winter. Redheads are similar in pattern to the larger Canvasbacks. The breeding female (top) and breeding male (bottom) are illustrated.

Ring-necked Duck, *Aythya collaris*
Family Anatidae (Ducks, Geese)
Size: 17"
Season: Winter
Habitat: Shallow lakes and ponds near woodlands, coastal bays

The Ring-necked Duck, also known as the Ring-billed Duck, is in the group of diving ducks that typically swim underwater to find plant and animal prey, although it may also behave like a dabbling duck and bob for food at the surface. This gregarious small duck looks tall, with its post-like head and neck and a peaked crown. The breeding male is stunning, with contrasting light and dark plumage and a dark metallic brown-purple head. The bill is gray, with a white ring and black tip, and the base of the bill is edged with white feathers. The female is more brownish overall, with white eye-rings. The ring around the neck, for which this duck is named, is actually a very inconspicuous brownish band at the bottom of the neck in the male bird. The breeding female (top) and breeding male (bottom) are illustrated.

Lesser Scaup, *Aythya affinis*
Family Anatidae (Ducks, Geese)
Size: 17"
Season: Winter
Habitat: Marshes, shallow lakes, coastal bays

The Lesser Scaup is a small, short-bodied duck with a tall head profile and a relatively thin bill. The breeding male is distinctly two-toned, with white sides, a variegated pale gray back, and a black rear and front. The head has a dark metallic violet or greenish cast in good light, and the bill has a small black dot at the nail. The nonbreeding male is paler, with brown on the sides. Females are gray-brown, with a dark brown head and a white patch at the base of the bill. This is a diving duck that forages for aquatic plants and insects. It is very similar to the Greater Scaup, but is smaller and has a more peaked head. The breeding female (top) and breeding male (bottom) are illustrated.

Bufflehead, *Bucephala albeola*
Family Anatidae (Ducks, Geese)
Size: 14"
Season: Winter
Habitat: Lakes, rivers, coastal bays

The Bufflehead is a diminutive diving duck; indeed, it is the smallest duck in North America. Also known as the Bumblebee Duck, it forms small flocks that forage in the open water for aquatic plants and invertebrates. The puffy, rounded head seems large for the body and compared to the small gray-blue bill. The breeding male is striking, with a large white patch on the back half of its head that contrasts with the black front of the head and back. The underside is white. The female is paler overall, with a dark gray-brown head and an airfoil-shaped white patch behind the eyes. Flight is low to the water, with rapid wing beats. The breeding female (top) and breeding male (bottom) are illustrated.

Red-breasted Merganser,
Mergus serrator
Family Anatidae (Ducks, Geese)
Size: 23"
Season: Winter in eastern Texas,
transient migrant elsewhere
Habitat: Lakes near woodlands, rivers, coastal areas

Mergansers are known as Fishing Ducks or Sawtooths. They dive and chase fish of considerable size underwater and secure their catch with a long, thin bill that is serrated along the edges. Both male and female Red-breasted Mergansers sport a fine, long, two-part crest. The male has a white band around the neck, a dark head, a red bill, and gray flanks. The female is grayish overall, with a brown head. The nonbreeding male closely resembles the female. Flight is low and quick on pointed wings. The breeding female (top) and breeding male (bottom) are illustrated.

DUCKS, GEESE

Ruddy Duck, *Oxyura jamaicencis*
Family Anatidae (Ducks, Geese)
Size: 15"
Season: Winter
Habitat: Open water, wetlands, bays

The Ruddy Duck is a member of the "stiff-tailed ducks," known for their rigid tail feathers that are often cocked up in display. It dives deep into the water for its food, which consists of aquatic vegetation, and flies low over the water with quick wing beats. It is a relatively small duck with a big head and a flat, broad body. The breeding male is rich sienna brown overall, with white cheeks, a black cap and nape, and a bright blue bill. The female is drab, with a conspicuous dark stripe across the cheek. Nonbreeding males become gray. The Ruddy Duck can sink low into the water, grebe-like, and will often dive to escape danger. The breeding female (top) and breeding male (bottom) are illustrated.

Plain Chachalaca,

Ortalis vetula
Family Cracidae (Chachalacas)
Size: 22"
Season: Year-round resident in southern Texas
Habitat: Tropical woods, thickets

The Plain Chachalaca is a Texas specialty; the lower Rio Grande valley being the only reliable place to find this bird in the United States. It is a chicken-like bird with a long tail, stout legs, and a small head. The plumage is very plain brown overall, with lighter, rufous-brown underparts and a gray head and neck. The bill is short and thick with a curved culmen, and along the side of the throat is a thin, red bare patch (not always visible in the field). The tail is glossy bluish-green with white tips. Chachalacas furtively travel in small groups, foraging in trees or on the ground for fruit and leaves. Their voice is like the name, a loud, grating chock-a-loc, often forming a cacophony when heard in unison with many individuals. The adult is illustrated.

Scaled Quail, *Callipepla squamata*

Family Odontophoridae (Quail)
Size: 10"
Season: Year-round resident in western Texas
Habitat: Dry, open grasslands and scrub

Also known as the Cottontop, the Scaled Quail is a plump, short-tailed ground bird with a tall, white-tipped crest. The upperparts and head are gray-brown, while the underparts and around the neck are paler with black-tipped feathers that create a scaled appearance. There is also white streaking along the flanks and the back edges of the tertials. Females generally have a shorter crest. Scaled Quail forage on the ground in large groups, or coveys, for insect and grains, and they usually run away rather than fly when alarmed. The voice is a two-part clucking, *pe-cos,* or a short shriek. The adult is illustrated.

Northern Bobwhite,
Colinus virginianus
Family Odontophoridae (Quail)
Size: 10"
Season: Year-round
Habitat: Brushy fields and open woodlands

The Bobwhite, like other quail, is a secretive, ground-dwelling bird that usually takes flight only if alarmed. It travels in coveys of ten or more, while scavenging for seeds, berries, and insects. It is plump with a very short, gray tail. Its plumage is heavily streaked rufous, gray, and black. It has a white superciliary stripe and throat. The female is paler with a greater extent of rufous coloring and buffy eye-lines and throat. Its call sounds somewhat like its name: *bob-white*. The illustration shows an adult.

Wild Turkey, *Meleagris gallopavo*
Family Phasianidae (Pheasants, Grouse, Turkeys)
Size: 36–48", male larger than female
Season: Year-round
Habitat: Open mixed woodlands

The Wild Turkey is a very large (though slimmer than the domestic variety), dark, ground-dwelling bird. The legs are thick and stout, and the heavily barred plumage is quite iridescent in strong light. The head and neck appear small for the body size and are covered with bluish, warty, crinkled bare skin that droops under the chin in a red wattle. Often foraging in flocks, they roam the ground for seeds, grubs, and insects and then roost at night in trees. Males emit the familiar *gobble,* while females are less vocal, making a soft clucking sound. In display, the male will hunch with its tail up and spread like a giant fan. Southwestern races, as in Texas, show white banding on the tail and uppertail coverts. The adult male is illustrated.

Common Loon, *Gavia immer*
Family Gaviidae (Loons)
Size: 24"
Season: Winter
Habitat: Coastal waters

Riding low in the water outside the surf zone, this heavy water-bird periodically dives for fish, propelled by its strong webbed feet. Designed for a life in the water, it has legs set far back on its body, which makes walking on land a clumsy affair and takeoff into the air labored. In Texas this bird is usually seen in its drab gray-and-white plumage, unlike the flashy black-and-white spotted plumage it sports during the summer in northern lakes. Its call is a haunting yodel, but not commonly heard while in Texas for the winter months. The Common Loon can be distinguished from other loons by the horizontal posture of its large bill (not held upward). It is fairly common in winter, scattered singly or in pairs along the coast. The nonbreeding adult is illustrated.

Eared Grebe, *Podiceps nigricollis*
Family Podicipedidae (Grebes)
Size: 13"
Season: Summer in northern Texas, winter elsewhere
Habitat: Shallow freshwater ponds and lakes

The Eared Grebe is a small, thin grebe with a narrow, pointed bill that turns up at the tip. The breeding adult has a black head, neck, and back, a pale belly, and rufous sides. The head has a peaked crown, bright red eyes, and golden-yellow ear tufts. In winter the birds have whitish head markings, breast, and sides, with no ear tufts. A clean white secondary patch can be seen on the wing in flight. The tail is tiny and hidden. Eared Grebes are gregarious, forming large nesting colonies, and forage by diving for aquatic invertebrates and insects. They are slightly more buoyant than other grebes. The breeding adult is illustrated.

Pied-billed Grebe,
Podilymbus podiceps
Family Podicipedidae (Grebes)
Size: 13"
Season: Year-round
Habitat: Freshwater ponds and lakes

The Pied-billed Grebe is a secretive small grebe that lurks in sheltered waters, diving for small fish, leeches, snails, and crawfish. When alarmed, or to avoid predatory snakes and hawks, it has the habit of sinking until only its head is above water, remaining that way until danger has passed. It is brownish overall and slightly darker above, with a tiny tail and short wings. The breeding adult has a conspicuous dark ring around the middle of the bill, which is missing in winter plumage. Pied-billed Grebes nest on a floating mat of vegetation. The breeding adult is illustrated.

Wood Stork, *Mycteria americana*
Family Ciconiidae (Storks)
Size: 40"
Season: Summer
Habitat: Freshwater ponds and lakes

The Wood Stork is a large, somewhat unattractive bird with a white body, black flight feathers, and a featherless neck and head covered in blackish, scaly skin. The bill is long, decurved, and blunt at its tip. It forms flocks and feeds by probing its bill into the mud, stirring up prey such as fish and snakes. It flies with its neck outstretched in loose, unorganized groups. At rest it will stand motionless for an hour or more in a distinctive, upright posture with its bill tucked down and against the body. It roosts in mangrove or cypress trees, and emits croaking sounds or chattering by snapping the upper and lower mandibles together. The illustration shows an adult.

Magnificent Frigatebird,
Fregata magnificens
Family Fregatidae (Frigatebirds)
Size: 40"
Season: Summer
Habitat: Gulf Coast

The Magnificent Frigatebird can be seen soaring effortlessly for hours, high in the air off the coast. To feed, it skims the surface of the water in flight to snatch fish, or may steal food from other seabirds. It has long, slender wings and a deeply forked tail. The bill is long and hooked. Males are black overall with a curious red throat patch that can be inflated like a balloon. Females have a white belly and sides. The illustration shows an adult female.

Neotropic Cormorant,
Phalacrocorax brasilianus
Family Phalacrocoracidae (Cormorants)
Size: 25"
Season: Year-round
Habitat: Shallow fresh or saltwater habitats

Also known as the Olivaceous Cormorant, the Neotropic Cormorant is a slender, small cormorant with a relatively long tail. It is glossy black overall, paler on the back and wings with black margins to the coverts and back feathers, giving a scaled look. There is a small, yellow gular pouch bordered by a thin line of white feathers, and the eyes are green. Breeding adults have more pronounced white feathering behind the gular pouch and white tufts at the ear region. Juveniles are browner and paler overall. Neotropic Cormorants dive for small fish, frogs, and invertebrates, and are often seen perching on branches or posts with wings outspread to dry their feathers. The breeding adult is illustrated.

Double-crested Cormorant,
Phalacrocorax auritus
Family Phalacrocoracidae (Cormorants)
Size: 32"
Season: Year-round near the coast, winter inland
Habitat: Open waters

Named for the two long white plumes that emerge from behind the eyes during breeding season, the Double-crested Cormorant is an expert swimmer that dives underwater to chase down fish. Because its plumage lacks the normal oils to repel water, it will stand with wings outstretched to dry itself. It is all black, with a pale glossy cast on the back and wings. The eyes are bright green, the bill is thin and hooked, and the throat patch and lores are yellow. The breeding adult is illustrated.

American White Pelican,
Pelecanus erythrorhynchos
Family Pelecanidae (Pelicans)
Size: 62"
Season: Winter, year-round on the southern coast
Habitat: Open fresh water

One of North America's largest birds, the American White Pelican has a wingspan of over 9 feet. It is white overall, with black flight feathers. The massive bill is orange and has a membranous, expandable throat pouch. In posture, it holds its neck in a characteristic strong kink and its folded wings in a peak along its back. American White Pelicans often feed in cooperative groups, herding fish as they swim and scooping them up by dipping their bills in the water. They never plunge-dive like the Brown Pelican. When breeding, a strange horny growth appears on the upper mandible in both sexes. The nonbreeding adult is illustrated.

Brown Pelican,

Pelecanus occidentalis
Family Pelecanidae (Pelicans)
Size: 50"
Season: Year-round
Habitat: Coastal waters

The majestic Brown Pelican enlivens the coastal waters with its spectacular feeding process of plunge-diving for fish, head-first, from some height. It often flies in formation inches from incoming swells, gaining lift and rarely needing to flap its wings. Plumage is a bleached gray-brown overall, with a white head and neck and a massive bill. In breeding plumage, the head is pale yellow with a brown-red nape patch and a black strip down the back of the neck. The Brown Pelican is quite gregarious, and nests in trees or in slight depressions in the sand or rocks. The breeding adult is illustrated.

American Bittern,

Botaurus lentiginosus
Family Ardeidae (Herons and Egrets)
Size: 27"
Season: Winter
Habitat: Marshy areas with dense vegetation

The American Bittern is a fairly large, secretive heron with a small head, a long, straight bill, and a thick body. It has a habit of standing still with its neck and bill pointed straight up to imitate the surrounding reeds. Its plumage is very cryptic: Above, it is variegated brown and tan, and below it is pale brown or whitish with thick rust-colored streaking that extends up the neck. The bill is yellow-green and dark on the upper mandible. A dark patch extends from the lower bill to the upper neck. The legs are yellow-green and thick. American Bitterns skulk slowly through reeds and grasses to catch frogs, insects, and invertebrates. The adult is illustrated.

Great Blue Heron,
Ardea herodias
Family Ardeidae (Herons, Egrets)
Size: 46"
Season: Year-round
Habitat: Most aquatic areas,
including lakes, creeks, and marshes

The Great Blue Heron is the largest heron in North America. Walking slowly through shallow water or fields, it stalks fish, crabs, and small vertebrates, catching them with its massive bill. With long legs and a long neck, it is blue-gray overall, with a white face and a heavy yellow-orange bill. The crown is black and supports plumes of medium length. The front of the neck is white, with distinct black chevrons fading into breast plumes. In flight, the neck is tucked back and the wing beats are regular and labored. The adult is illustrated.

Great Egret, *Ardea alba*
Family Ardeidae (Herons, Egrets)
Size: 38"
Season: Year-round
Habitat: Freshwater and
saltwater marshes

The Great Egret is all white and has a long, thin yellow bill and long black legs. It develops long, lacy plumes across its back during the breeding season. Stalking slowly, it pursues fish, frogs, and other aquatic animals. The adult is illustrated.

Snowy Egret,
Egretta thula
Family Ardeidae (Herons, Egrets)
Size: 24"
Season: Year-round
Habitat: Open water, marshes, swamps

The Snowy Egret is all white, with lacy plumes across the back in breeding season. The bill is slim and black, and the legs are black with bright yellow feet. The juvenile has greenish legs with a yellow stripe along the front. The Snowy Egret forages for fish and frogs along the shore by moving quickly, shuffling to stir up prey, which it then stabs with its bill. Sometimes it may run to pursue its prey. The name of this bird can be remembered by keeping in mind that it wears yellow "boots" because it is cold or "snowy." The breeding adult is illustrated.

Little Blue Heron,
Egretta caerulea
Family Ardeidae (Herons, Egrets)
Size: 25"
Season: Year-round
Habitat: Freshwater or coastal swamps

The Little Blue Heron is a medium-size heron that skulks along shorelines with vegetative cover, often using its wings to cast a shadow over the water to see and attract fish. It is overall slate blue with a purple cast on the neck. The bill is pale gray with a dark tip, and the legs are greenish. The juvenile is all white with small dark tips on the primaries, and it can be confused with other white herons. The illustration shows an adult.

Tricolored Heron,
Egretta tricolor
Family Ardeidae
(Herons, Egrets)
Size: 26"
Season: Year-round
Habitat: Coastal marshes

The Tricolored Heron is a thin, bluish-gray heron with a white belly and brownish neck stripe and lower back. In nonbreeding plumage, it has yellow lores and an orangey bill, but in breeding season this area of the lores and bill are blue and the bill has a dark tip. It also develops plumes behind the ears and across the lower back. To feed, it will actively pursue prey or stand motionless, waiting to stab a fish or frog with its thin, spear-like bill. The illustration shows a breeding adult.

Reddish Egret,
Egretta rufescens
Family Ardeidae (Herons, Egrets)
Size: 26"
Season: Year-round
Habitat: Coastal marshes

The Reddish Egret is thick-necked and has two color morphs: an all-white version and the more common dark version. The dark morph is gray with a rusty-reddish neck lined with stringy coarse feathers that give it a disheveled look. The bill is long and powerful, and pinkish with a black tip. A quite active bird, it often runs through the shallows and chases after fish like a maniac. It also employs the technique of creating an area of shade with its outstretched wings to attract fish and see them better. It is usually solitary. The illustration shows an adult.

Cattle Egret,
Bubulcus ibis
Family Ardeidae (Herons, Egrets)
Size: 20"
Season: Year-round
Habitat: Upland fields,
often near cattle in grazing land

The Cattle Egret is a widespread species originally from Africa and now quite common in the southern United States. Unlike most herons, it is not normally found in aquatic environments. It forms groups around cattle, often perching atop them, and feeds on insects aroused by the movement of their hooves. It is stocky and all white with a comparatively short yellow bill and short black legs. In breeding plumage, the legs and bill turn a bright orange, and a peachy, pale yellow forms on the crown, breast, and back. The illustration shows a nonbreeding adult.

Green Heron, *Butorides virensens*
Family Ardeidae (Herons, Egrets)
Size: 18"
Season: Year-round along the coast,
summer inland
Habitat: Ponds, creeks, wetlands

The Green Heron is a compact, crow-size heron that perches on low branches over the water, crouching forward to search for fish, snails, and insects. It is known to toss a bug into the water to attract fish. The Green Heron is really not so green, but rather a dull grayish-blue with a burgundy-chestnut-colored neck and black crown. The bill is dark, and the legs are bright yellow-orange. When disturbed, its crest feathers will rise, and it will stand erect and twitch its tail. It is fairly secretive and solitary. The adult is illustrated.

Black-crowned Night-Heron, *Nycticorax nycticorax*
Family Ardeidae (Herons, Egrets)
Size: 25"
Season: Year-round along the coast, summer inland
Habitat: Marshes, swamps with wooded banks

The nocturnal Black-crowned Night-Heron is a stocky, thick-necked heron with a comparatively large head and a sharp, heavy, thick bill. It has pale gray wings, white underparts, and a black crown, back, and bill. The eyes are piercing red, and the legs are yellow. In breeding plumage, it develops long white plumes on the rear of the head. During the day it roosts in groups, but at night it forages alone, waiting motionless for prey such as fish or crabs. It may even raid the nests of other birds. Its voice is composed of low-pitched barks and croaks. The adult is illustrated.

Yellow-crowned Night-Heron,
Nyctanassa violacea
Family Ardeidae (Herons, Egrets)
Size: 24"
Season: Year-round along the coast, summer inland
Habitat: Marshes, swamps with wooded banks

Shaped somewhat like the Black-crowned Night-Heron, the Yellow-crowned Night-Heron is blue-gray overall with a black face, white cheek patch, and slim, pale crown that is not really yellow but whitish or pale buff. In breeding plumage, it develops plumes from behind the crest. Its eyes are large and red, and its legs are yellow. The immature bird is drab brown-gray, mottled with light streaks. It is nocturnal, but will occasionally feed during the day for crustaceans and other aquatic animals, roosting in groups at night. The illustration shows an adult.

White-faced Ibis, *Plegadis chihi*
Family Threskiornithidae (Ibises)
Size: 23"
Season: Year-round along the coast, transient migrant elsewhere
Habitat: Swamps, shallows of freshwater lakes, fields

IBISES

The White-faced Ibis is somewhat heron-like in shape, with a relatively short neck and a long, downcurved grayish bill. The plumage is dark metallic green-black on the wings and back, with a dark chestnut body, neck, and head. The lores are reddish and bordered with white feathers that encircle the dark red eyes. In winter, adults of both sexes are all dark with pale streaking on the head and neck, and they lack the white feathers around the eye. Breeding adults have bright red legs. Unlike herons, ibises fly with their necks extended. They walk steadily while picking and probing with their long bills for aquatic invertebrates, and they roost in trees. The breeding adult is illustrated.

Roseate Spoonbill,
Platalea ajaja
Family Threskiornithidae (Ibises)
Size: 32"
Season: Year-round along the coast
Habitat: Shallow saltwater wetlands, agricultural fields

The roseate spoonbill is easily identified by its unique feeding technique. It swings its bill from side to side in shallow water or mud to catch fish, shrimp, and other small aquatic life. Unlike the heron, it constantly moves forward and seldom remains stationary. Its body is pink with red in the shoulders; its neck is white and tail is orange. Its face is pale green-gray bordered by a black feathered patch. The bill is very long, thick at the base then thinning to a compressed spatula shape. The spoonbill flies with its neck outstretched. While resting, it will stand on one leg for considerable lengths of time. The illustration shows an adult.

Black Vulture,
Coragyps atratus
Family Cathartidae (New World Vultures)
Size: 25"
Season: Year-round
Habitat: Open, dry country

Like the Turkey Vulture, the Black Vulture is adept at soaring. Its wing beats, however, are faster, and while soaring, it holds its wings at a flat angle instead of a dihedral. It is stocky in physique, has a short, stubby tail, and shorter wings than the Turkey Vulture. The primaries are pale on an otherwise black body, and the head is bald and gray. It eats carrion and garbage and is quite aggressive at feeding sites. The illustration shows an adult.

Turkey Vulture,
Cathartes aura
Family Cathartidae (New World Vultures)
Size: 27"
Season: Year-round or summer
Habitat: Open, dry country

The Turkey Vulture is known for its effortless, skilled soaring. It will often soar for hours, without flapping, rocking in the breeze on 6-foot wings that form an upright V shape, or dihedral angle. It has a black body and inner wing, with pale flight feathers and tail feathers that give it a noticeable two-toned appearance from below. The tail is longish, and the feet extend no more than halfway past the base of the tail. The head is naked, red, and small, so the bird appears almost headless in flight. The bill is strongly hooked to aid in tearing apart its favored prey, carrion. Juveniles have a dark gray head. Turkey Vultures often roost in flocks and form groups around food or at a roadkill site. The adult is illustrated.

Osprey, *Pandion haliaetus*
Family Pandionidae (Osprey)
Size: 23", female larger than male
Season: Transient migrant and winter
Habitat: Always near water,
salt or fresh

Also known as the Fish Hawk, the Osprey exhibits a dramatic feeding method, plunging feet-first into the water to snag fish. Sometimes it completely submerges itself, then laboriously flies off with its heavy catch. It is dark brown above and white below, and has distinct dark eye-stripes contiguous with the nape. Females show a dark, mottled "necklace" across the breast, and juveniles have pale streaking on the back. The Osprey flies with an obvious crook at the wrist, appearing gull-like, and its wings are long and narrow, with a dark carpal patch. The adult is illustrated.

White-tailed Kite, *Elanus leucurus*
Family Accipitridae (Hawks, Eagles)
Size: 15"
Season: Year-round
Habitat: Open grasslands with trees or thickets, roadsides

The White-tailed Kite, also known as the Black-shouldered Kite, is an elegant kite with long, pointed wings, a long tail, and a small, hooked bill. It is gray above, with a large black shoulder patch and a white tail. The underside and head are white, with gray on the nape and black around the red eyes, giving an angry expression. Juveniles have brown streaking across the neck and on the crown. White-tailed Kites fly with a slight dihedral angle to the wings, and they have a black spot at the wrist on the underwing. They patrol grasslands in the air or from a perch, and hover before attacking their prey of rodents and reptiles. The adult is illustrated.

Bald Eagle,
Haliaeetus leucocephalus
Family Accipitridae (Hawks, Eagles)
Size: 30–40", female larger than male
Season: Year-round in eastern Texas, winter elsewhere
Habitat: Lakes, rivers with tall perches or cliffs

The Bald Eagle is a large raptor that is widespread but fairly uncommon. It eats fish or scavenges dead animals, and congregates in large numbers where food is abundant. Its plumage is dark brown, contrasting with its white head and tail. Juveniles show white splotching across the wings and breast. The yellow bill is large and powerful, and the talons are large and sharp. In flight, it holds its wings fairly flat and straight, resembling a long plank. Bald Eagles make huge nests of sticks high in trees. The adult is illustrated.

Sharp-shinned Hawk,
Accipiter striatus
Family Accipitridae (Hawks, Eagles)
Size: 10–14", female larger than male
Season: Winter or year-round
Habitat: Woodlands, bushy areas

The Sharp-shinned Hawk is North America's smallest accipiter, with a longish, squared tail and stubby, rounded wings. Its short wings allow for agile flight in tight, wooded quarters, where it quickly attacks small birds in flight. It is grayish above and light below, barred with pale rufous stripes. The eyes are set forward on the face to aid in the direct pursuit of prey. The juvenile is white below, streaked with brown. The similar Cooper's Hawk is larger with a longer, rounded tail, and more often hunts in open country. The adult is illustrated.

Red-shouldered Hawk,
Buteo lineatus
Family Accipitridae (Hawks, Eagles)
Size: 17"
Season: Year-round
Habitat: Wooded areas near water

The Red-shouldered Hawk is a solitary, small, accipiter-like buteo with a long tail. It waits patiently on its perch before flying down to attack a variety of small animals. It has a banded black-and-white tail and spotted dark wings. The head and shoulder are rust colored, while the breast is light with rust barring. The legs are long and yellow, and the bill is hooked. In flight, there is a pale arc just inside the wing tips, and it flaps its wings with quick beats followed by short glides. Western populations are darker overall than their eastern counterparts. The adult is illustrated.

White-Tailed Hawk,
Buteo albicaudatus
Family Accipitridae (Hawks, Eagles)
Size: 20-23", females larger than males
Season: Year-round in southeast Texas
Habitat: Coastal plains, grasslands

A Texas specialty, the White-tailed Hawk is a stocky buteo with long, narrow wings and a short, white tail with a black subterminal band. The head and back are slate gray, the wings are dark gray, and the shoulder region is rust colored. The throat and underparts are white in the adult, but juvenile birds show dark barring on the belly and have a dark throat. From a perch or from flight, White-tailed Hawks capture insects and small vertebrates in the grass or scrub. They may also hunt at the edges of grassland fires where prey is scattering from the flames.

Red-tailed Hawk,
Buteo jamaicensis
Family Accipitridae (Hawks, Eagles)
Size: 20"
Season: Year-round
Habitat: Open country, prairies

This widespread species is the most common buteo in the United States. It has broad, rounded wings and a stout, hooked bill. Its plumage is highly variable depending on geographic location. In general, the underparts are light with darker streaking that forms a dark band across the belly, the upperparts are dark brown, and the tail is rufous. Light spotting occurs along the scapulars. In flight, there is a noticeable dark patch along the inner leading edge of the underwing. Red-tailed Hawks glide down from perches, such as telephone poles and posts in open country, to catch rodents, and they may also hover to spot prey. They are usually seen alone or in pairs. Voice is the familiar *keeer!* The western adult is illustrated.

Swainson's Hawk, *Buteo swainsoni*
Family Accipitridae (Hawks, Eagles)
Size: 19", females larger than males
Season: Summer
Habitat: Dry prairies, open fields

The Swainson's Hawk is a buteo with a long tail, long wings with pointed tips, and a relatively small, rounded head. It has variable plumage colors, ranging from dark morphs to the more common light morphs. The light morph has a white underside, a dark brown back, a rufous breast, and white lores and chin. Darker forms become rufous or dark brown on the breast and belly. In flight, the light morph has pale wing linings and a pale belly that contrasts with its darker flight feathers and tail. Swainson's Hawks feed on small mammals, insects, and reptiles, either descending from a perch or by stalking on the ground. The hawk's voice is a high-pitched *eeeeww*.

American Kestrel,
Falco sparverius
Family Falconidae (Falcons)
Size: 10"
Season: Year-round
Habitat: Open country,
urban areas

North America's most common falcon, the American Kestrel is a tiny, robin-size falcon with long, pointed wings and tail. Fast in flight, it hovers above fields or dives from its perch on branches or a wire to capture small animals and insects. The upperparts are rufous and barred with black, the wings are blue-gray, and the breast is buff or white and streaked with black spots. The head is patterned with a gray crown and vertical patches of black down the face. The female has rufous wings and a barred tail. Also known as the Sparrow Hawk, it has a habit of flicking its tail up and down while perched. The adult male is illustrated.

Crested Caracara,
Caracara cheriway
Family Falconidae (Falcons)
Size: 23"
Season: Year-round
Habitat: Dry prairies and scrubland

The Northern Caracara is a falcon that is somewhat vulture-like in its behavior. It forages on carcasses or immobile prey, which it finds by soaring on flat wings or cruising over pastures and open savanna. It may also perch on poles or on the ground. Its head seems large for its body and it has a long neck and long legs. It is an overall dark bird with a white neck, black cap, and large, hooked bill. The face has a large patch of reddish bare skin. In flight the white wing tips and tail are distinctive. This tropical falcon is rare in the United States and was once a threatened species here. The illustration shows an adult.

Common Moorhen,
Gallinula chloropus
Family Rallidae (Rails, Coots)
Size: 14"
Season: Year-round near the coast, summer inland
Habitat: Freshwater ponds and wetlands

The Common Moorhen, like the American Coot, is a type of rail that behaves more like a duck. It paddles along, bobbing its head up and down, picking at the water surface for any small aquatic animals, insects, or plants. Having short wings, it is a poor flier, but its very long toes allow it to walk on floating vegetation. It is overall dark gray, with a brownish back, black head, and white areas on the tail and sides. In breeding plumage, the forehead shield is deep red and the bill is red with a yellow tip. It is also known as the Common Gallinule. The breeding adult is illustrated.

American Coot, *Fulica americana*
Family Rallidae (Rails, Coots)
Size: 15"
Season: Year-round
Habitat: Wetlands, ponds, urban lawns and parks

The American Coot has a plump body and a thick head and neck. It is a very common bird and becomes relatively tame in urban areas and parks. It dives for fish to feed, but it will also dabble like a duck or pick food from the ground. It is dark gray overall, with a black head and white bill that ends with a dark narrow ring. The white trailing edge of the wings can be seen in flight. The toes are flanked with lobes that enable the coot to walk on water plants and swim efficiently. Juveniles are similar in plumage to adults but paler. Coots are often seen in very large flocks. The adult is illustrated.

Clapper Rail, *Rallus longirostris*
Family Rallidae (Rails, Coots)
Size: 14"
Season: Year-round
Habitat: Coastal salt water or
brackish marshes

Also known as the Marsh Hen, the Clapper Rail is very shy and difficult to see. It lurks through marshy vegetation and usually chooses to walk or swim rather than fly. It forages by probing through mud and grass for a variety of small prey, vocalizing harsh, clattering *kek-kek-kek* sounds in rapid succession. It is a relatively thin rail with a long, slightly decurved bill. The plumage is gray-brown above with a pale rust breast and barred flanks. The illustration shows an adult.

CRANES

Whooping Crane, *Grus americana*
Family Gruidae (Cranes)
Size: 54"
Season: Winter
Habitat: Saltwater marshes and
fields of the Aransas National Wildlife Refuge

The extremely rare Whooping Crane, North America's tallest bird, has been brought back from the brink of extinction by extensive conservation efforts. It is a huge, long-legged crane with a loose bustle of tertial feathers and a long, heron-like neck and long bill. The plumage is all white except for black primaries. The head has patches of bare, red skin on the crown and malar region, with black feathering on the latter. Juveniles show brown across the back and head. Whooping Cranes forage in the shallow water and dry fields for a wide variety of prey, including grains, shellfish, insects, and small vertebrates. The voice is a high, resonant, trumpeting call, often heard in unison with another individual. Cranes fly with the neck and legs extended. The adult is illustrated.

Sandhill Crane,
Grus canadensis
Family Gruidae (Cranes)
Size: 45"
Season: Winter
Habitat: Fields, shallow wetlands

The Sandhill Crane is a tall bird with long, strong legs, a long neck, and a long, straight bill. The long, thick tertial feathers create the distinctive bustle on the rear of all cranes. The top of the head is covered by bare red skin. Plumage is gray overall but may become spotted with rust-colored stains caused by preening with a bill stained by iron-rich mud. In flocks, it grazes in fields, gleaning grains, insects, and small animals, and returns to protected wetland areas in the evening to roost. The voice of the Sandhill Crane is a throaty, penetrating trumpeting sound. Unlike herons, it flies in groups with its neck extended. The adult is illustrated.

Black-bellied Plover,
Pluvialis squatarola
Family Charadriidae (Plovers)
Size: 11"
Season: Winter
Habitat: Open areas, coastal or inland

The Black-bellied Plover is a relatively large plover with long, pointed wings and a whistling flight call. Like other plovers, it feeds by scooting quickly along the ground, stopping suddenly to peck at small prey in the mud or sand, and then scooting along again. Its winter plumage is gray above and paler below, with a white belly. The bill is black, short, and thick. A distinctive black patch on the axillary feathers can be seen in flight. In breeding plumage, it develops the sharply contrasting black belly, face, and front of neck. The nonbreeding adult (top) and breeding adult (bottom) are illustrated.

Semipalmated Plover,

Charadrius semipalmatus
Family Charadriidae (Plovers)
Size: 7"
Season: Winter
Habitat: Open sand and mudflats,
coastal beaches

The Semipalmated Plover is a small, plump plover with pointed wings, large black eyes, and a relatively large, rounded head. It has a dark brown back and crown, is white below, and has a small orange bill with a dark tip. The head has dark bands across the eyes and around the neck. The legs and feet are yellow. Winter and breeding plumages are similar, with the exception of an all-dark bill and lighter supercilium in winter. This widespread plover flies in flocks but disperses to feed, which entails fast running interrupted by sudden stops to probe for invertebrates. Its name is derived from the partial webbing at the base of the toes. The breeding adult is illustrated.

Killdeer, *Charadrius vociferus*

Family Charadriidae (Plovers)
Size: 10"
Season: Year-round
Habitat: Inland fields, farmlands,
lakeshores, meadows

The Killdeer gets its name from its piercing *kill-dee* call, which is often heard before these well-camouflaged plovers are seen. Well adapted to human-altered environments, it is quite wide-spread and gregarious. It has long, pointed wings, a long tail, and a conspicuous double-banded breast. The upper parts are dark brown, the belly is white, and the head is patterned with a white supercilium and forehead. The tail is rusty orange with a black tip. In flight, there is a noticeable white stripe across the flight feathers. The Killdeer is known for the classic "broken wing" display that it uses to distract predators from its nest and young. The adult is illustrated.

American Oystercatcher,
Haematopus palliatus
Family Haematopodidae
(Oystercatchers)
Size: 18"
Season: Year-round
Habitat: Coastal beaches, tide pools

The American Oystercatcher is a chunky, short-tailed, and short-winged shorebird with a dark brown back, white belly, and black head. It has a heavy, knife-like, bright red bill, yellow eyes, and stocky, salmon-colored legs. In flight there is a distinct white bar across the secondary feathers. It follows the tidal pattern, foraging at low tide and roosting at high tide in groups with other shorebirds and gulls. It uses its bill to pry away shellfish—including oysters—from rocks, or to probe for worms. The bill is also used to jam open bivalves and devour the flesh. Its voice is a loud, piping call. The illustration shows an adult.

American Avocet,
Recurvirostra americana
Family Recurvirostridae (Avocets, Stilts)
Size: 18"
Season: Year-round along Gulf Coast,
summer in northwest Texas
Habitat: Shallow wetlands, marshes

The elegant American Avocet has a long, delicate, upturned black bill and long, thin blue-gray legs. The upperparts are patterned black and white, the belly is white, and the head and neck is light orange-brown punctuated by black eyes. The bill of the female is slightly shorter than that of the male and has a greater bend. Nonbreeding adults have a pale gray head and neck. Avocets use a side-to-side sweeping motion of the bill to stir up small crustaceans and insect larvae as they wade methodically through the shallows. They may even submerge their heads as the water deepens. They are adept swimmers and emit a *wheet!* call in alarm. The breeding female (top) and breeding male (bottom) are illustrated.

Black-necked Stilt,
Himantopus mexicanus
Family Recurvirostridae (Avocets, Stilts)
Size: 14"
Season: Year-round along the Gulf Coast, summer in northwestern Texas
Habitat: Shallow wetlands, marshes, lagoons

The Black-necked Stilt looks like a tiny body on stilts. It has extremely long, delicate red legs and a thin, straight, needlelike black bill. The wings and mantle are black, and the underparts and tail are white. The head is dark above, with a white patch above the eyes. The female has a slightly lighter, brownish back. In flight, the long legs dangle behind the bird. To forage, it strides along to pick small prey from the water or vegetation, and it may voice a strident, barking *kek!* in alarm. Stilts are also known to perform the broken wing or broken leg act to distract predators. The adult male is illustrated.

Willet, *Catoptrophorus semipalmatus*
Family Scolopacidae (Sandpipers, Phalaropes)
Size: 15"
Season: Year-round
Habitat: Saltwater and freshwater wetlands, coastal beaches

The Willet is a heavy shorebird with a stout bill and conspicuous black-and-white wing markings in flight. Plumage is overall mocha brown above and pale below, with extensive mottling in the breeding season. It has white lores and eye-rings, and its plain gray legs are thick and sturdy. The Willet is found singly or in scattered flocks, and picks or probes for crabs, crustaceans, and worms in the mud and sand. Its call is a loud *wil-let*, often uttered in flight. The winter adult is illustrated.

Spotted Sandpiper,
Actitus macularius
Family Scolopacidae (Sandpipers, Phalaropes)
Size: 7.5"
Season: Winter
Habitat: Streamsides, edges of lakes and ponds

The solitary Spotted Sandpiper is known for its exaggerated, constant bobbing motion. It has a compact body, long tail, and short neck and legs. Plumage is brown above and light below, with a white shoulder patch. There are white eye-rings and superciliary stripe above the dark eye-lines. In breeding plumage, it develops heavy spotting from the chin to lower flanks and barring on the back. The bill is orange, with a dark tip. It has short wings, and in flight the thin white stripe on the upper wing can be seen. To forage, it teeters about, picking small water prey and insects from the shoreline. The breeding adult is illustrated.

Long-billed Curlew,
Numenius americanus
Family Scolopacidae (Sandpipers, Phalaropes)
Size: 23"
Season: Winter
Habitat: Open grasslands, coastal mudflats, and beaches

SANDPIPERS, PHALAROPES

Sometimes called the "Sicklebill," the Long-billed Curlew is North America's largest curlew. It has an extremely long, thin, decurved bill (longer in females than in males) and is mottled gray-brown above with buff underparts. The facial markings are not pronounced, and the undersides of the wings are a rich cinnamon color. It strides in a deliberate manner with its head forward, picking or probing for crustaceans and insects, and its large eyes enable it to feed in the dark hours of early morning. Voice is a loud, ringing *kur-lee!* Long-billed Curlews may form flocks with Whimbrels and Godwits during the winter months. The adult is illustrated.

Marbled Godwit, *Limosa fedoa*
Family Scolopacidae (Sandpipers, Phalaropes)
Size: 18"
Season: Winter
Habitat: Coastal beaches, mudflats, marshes

As its name suggests, the Marbled Godwit is marbled, or barred, with dark across its buff body, although the underside lacks marbling in winter plumage. The long pinkish bill has a slight upcurved portion at the tip, where it becomes dark in color. The legs are dark, and the underwing is a rich cinnamon color. It also has a light superciliary stripe above dark eye-lines. Marbled Godwits move about with slow, steady progress and probe in shallow water to find polychaete worms and crustaceans. Call is a loud *god-WIT*. The nonbreeding adult is illustrated.

Ruddy Turnstone,
Arenaria interpres
Family Scolopacidae (Sandpipers, Phalaropes)
Size: 9.5"
Season: Winter
Habitat: Wide variety of shoreline habitats, from rocky intertidal to beaches and mudflats

The gregarious, frenetic Ruddy Turnstone is a chunky, short-legged shorebird with a short, wedge-shaped bill. The breeding adult has ruddy and black upperparts, a white belly, and a complex pattern of black and white on the head. The nonbreeding bird is pale brown and black above, with drab head markings. The stubby legs are orange. In flight, the bird is white below and strongly patterned light and dark above. Turnstones bustle about constantly to pick, pry, or probe for almost any food item. Indeed, it will "turn stones" to search for its prey. The nonbreeding adult (top) and breeding adult (bottom) are illustrated.

Sanderling, *Calidris alba*
Family Scolopacidae (Sandpipers, Phalaropes)
Size: 8"
Season: Winter
Habitat: Coastal beaches, mudflats

The Sanderling is a common shorebird that runs back and forth following the incoming and outgoing surf, grabbing small invertebrates exposed by the waves. It is a small, active, squat sandpiper with a short bill and legs. In nonbreeding plumage, it is very pale above and white below, contrasting with the black legs and bill. There is a distinct black shoulder and leading edge of the wing. Females in breeding plumage are speckled brown above, while males develop rufous on the back, head, and neck. In flight, a white stripe on the upper wing is visible. Sanderlings may form large foraging flocks and even larger flocks while roosting. The nonbreeding adult is illustrated.

Dunlin, *Calidris alpina*
Family Scolopacidae (Sandpipers, Phalaropes)
Size: 8.5"
Season: Winter
Habitat: Coastal beaches, mudflats

This bird's name comes from the word "dun," which, meaning dull gray-brown in color, describes the winter plumage of the Dunlin. It is a rather small sandpiper with a long bill that droops down at the tip. In breeding plumage, there is a black belly patch and rufous tones on the back. In flight, a white stripe on the upper wing and a white rump separated by a central dark line can be seen. It forms huge flocks, swirling and circling in unison. The Dunlin walks steadily through shallow waters to feed, probing or picking crustaceans and other invertebrates. The nonbreeding adult (top) and breeding adult (bottom) are illustrated.

Western Sandpiper,
Calidris mauri
Family Scolopacidae (Sandpipers, Phalaropes)
Size: 6.5"
Season: Winter
Habitat: Saltwater and freshwater wetlands, mudflats, coastal beaches

The Western Sandpiper is one of the "peeps," or very small sandpipers. It has a relatively long black bill that droops slightly and black legs. In winter, it is pale gray-brown above and white below. In breeding plumage, there is rufous on the scapulars and face and much darker streaking on the breast and back. A thin white stripe on the upper wing is visible in flight, along with a white rump with a dark central stripe. Western Sandpipers feed in shallow water or at the tide line, probing or picking invertebrates and insects. They often form rather large flocks. The nonbreeding adult (top) and breeding adult (bottom) are illustrated.

Wilson's Snipe, *Gallinago delicata*
Family Scolopacidae (Sandpipers, Phalaropes)
Size: 10.5"
Season: Winter
Habitat: Saltwater and freshwater marshes

Previously known as the Common Snipe (a Eurasian species), the Wilson's Snipe is a cryptically marked, short-necked shorebird with a long, straight bill. The head is striped, and the back is flanked with white stripes bordering the scapulars. The underside is white, with extensive black barring, and the legs are short and pale greenish yellow. Plumage is similar in all seasons. While feeding, snipes probe rhythmically and deeply into the muddy substrate to extract worms, insect larvae, and crustaceans. It voices a loud *skipe!* when alarmed, or a *whit-whit-whit-whit*. Secretive and solitary, it will abruptly lift into flight when alarmed. Its flight is erratic and zigzagging and includes displays of "winnowing," where air across the tail feathers whistles during a steep descent. The adult is illustrated.

Bonaparte's Gull,
Chroicocephalus philadelphia
Family Laridae (Gulls, Terns)
Size: 13"
Season: Winter
Habitat: Coastal in winter, comes inland during migration

The Bonaparte's Gull is a small gull named after an American ornithologist who was related to Napoleon. It is agile and tern-like in flight, skimming low over the water to snatch fish. It has a thin, sharp black bill and red legs. Plumage in breeding season includes a black head that contrasts with its white body, and light gray back and wings. The primaries form a white triangle against the dark trailing edge when in flight. The nonbreeding adult has a mostly white head, with black eyes and small dark spots around the ears. A solitary gull, it does not form large flocks. Bonaparte's Gulls build nests made of sticks in evergreen trees. The nonbreeding adult (top) and breeding adult (bottom) are illustrated.

Laughing Gull,
Leucophaeus atricilla
Family Laridae (Gulls, Terns)
Size: 16"
Season: Year-round
Habitat: Coastal beaches and marshes, urban environments, pastures

The Laughing Gull is so named because of its loud, often incessant, laughing squawk. Social and uninhibited, it is a relatively thin, medium-size gull with long, pointed wings. The breeding adult has a black head with white eye arcs and a dark red bill. Upperparts are dark gray, underparts are white, and wing tips are black with small white dots at the ends. The nonbreeding adult has a white head with faint dark smudging behind the eye. Laughing Gulls eat crabs, fish, and worms, and will scavenge from humans for food or even steal from other birds. The illustration shows a breeding adult, below, and a nonbreeding adult, above.

Ring-billed Gull,
Larus delawarensis
Family Laridae (Gulls, Terns)
Size: 18"
Season: Winter
Habitat: Widespread from coast to inland lakes, ponds, and parking lots

The Ring-billed Gull is common and quite tame. It is a relatively small gull with a rounded white head and a yellow bill with a dark subterminal ring. It has a pale gray back with black primaries tipped with white, and white underparts. The eyes are pale yellow, and the legs are yellow. The nonbreeding adult has faint streaking on the nape and around the eyes. Ring-billed Gulls feed on the water or on the ground, taking a wide variety of food, and may scavenge in urban areas and dumps. The nonbreeding adult is illustrated.

Herring Gull, *Larus argentatus*
Family Laridae (Gulls, Terns)
Size: 25"
Season: Winter
Habitat: Wetlands, coastal beaches, fields

The widespread Herring Gull occurs across the North American continent. It is a large, relatively thin, white-headed gull with a pale gray back and white underparts. The bill is thick and yellow, with a reddish spot at the tip of the lower mandible. The primaries are black with white-spotted tips. The nonbreeding adult has brown streaking across the nape and neck. The legs are pink, and the eyes are pale yellow to ivory colored. Herring Gulls are opportunistic feeders, eating fish, worms, crumbs, and trash. They are known to drop shellfish from the air to crack open their shells. The nonbreeding adult (top) and breeding adult (bottom) are illustrated.

Caspian Tern, *Sterna caspia*
Family Laridae (Gulls, Terns)
Size: 21"
Season: Year-round along the Gulf Coast,
inland during migration
Habitat: Coastal and inland lakes
and rivers

The Caspian Tern is a very large, thick-necked tern, the size of a big gull. It has a pointed, rich red bill that is dark at the tip, and a black cap on its head. The upperparts are very pale gray, the underparts are white, and the primary feathers are pale gray above and tipped with dark on the underside. The legs are short and black. Nonbreeding adults have pale streaks through the cap. In flight, the Caspian Tern uses ponderous, shallow wing beats and is less agile than smaller terns. It flies above the water surface searching for prey, plunging headfirst to snatch small fish, and may rob food from other birds. Its voice is a harsh *craw!* The breeding adult is illustrated.

Forster's Tern, *Sterna forsteri*
Family Laridae (Gulls, Terns)
Size: 14"
Season: Year-round
Habitat: Coastal areas, lakes, marshes

The Forster's Tern is a medium-size tern with no crest and a relatively long, pointed orange bill with a black tip. Breeding plumage is very pale gray above and white below, with a forked white tail and very light primaries. The head has a black cap, and the short legs are red. Nonbreeding adults have darker primaries, a black ear patch in place of the cap, and an all-black bill. Forster's Terns display swallow-like flight, with narrow pointed wings, and they plunge-dive for fish. They voice short, harsh, one-syllable calls. The nonbreeding adult (top) and breeding adult (bottom) are illustrated.

Royal Tern,
Thalasseus maximus
Family Laridae (Gulls, Terns)
Size: 20"
Season: Year-round
Habitat: Sandy coastal shores

The Royal Tern is a large but sleek tern with pointed, thin wings, a black, crested cap and a red-orange, pointed bill. It is pale gray above and white below, with black legs. The non-breeding adult has limited dark on the head, often reduced to a dark patch just behind the eyes. The dark outer primaries are visible in flight. Like the Caspian Tern, the Royal Tern flies over the water surface, often hovering, then plunging down to catch fish. It breeds on sandbars in the company of thousands of other birds. The breeding adult (bottom) and nonbreeding adult (top) are illustrated.

Least Tern, *Sterna antillarum*
Family Laridae (Gulls, Terns)
Size: 9"
Season: Summer
Habitat: Sandy coastal shores

The Least Tern is the smallest North American tern, and the only tern with a yellow bill and legs. It has a black cap and white forehead patch, and is pale gray above and white below. The tail is forked, and the bill is tipped with black. Nonbreeding adults have a dark bill and increased white on the front of the cap. In flight, the wings are relatively narrow and a black bar can be seen on the outer primaries. Least Terns often hover over the water before plunge-diving to catch small fish. They also pick worms and insects from the ground. This sensitive bird was once threatened by development of its sandy coastal breeding grounds. The breeding adult is illustrated.

Black Skimmer, *Rynchops niger*
Family Laridae (Gulls, Terns)
Size: 18"
Season: Year-round along the Gulf Coast
Habitat: Coastal bays, estuaries, inland freshwater rivers and lakes

The Black Skimmer has a unique bill in that the lower mandible is substantially longer than the upper. The red bill is also thick at the base and knife-thin toward the end. This aids in the foraging practice of flying just above the water surface, wings held above the body, with the mouth open and the lower mandible cutting a furrow through the water. When the skimmer encounters something solid, its mouth slams shut and it hopefully acquires a fish. Plumage is black on the back, wings, and crown, and white below. The legs are tiny and red. Nonbreeding adults have a white nape, contiguous with the white of the body. The breeding adult is illustrated.

Mourning Dove, *Zenaida macroura*
Family Columbidae (Pigeons, Doves)
Size: 12"
Season: Year-round
Habitat: Open brushy areas, urban areas

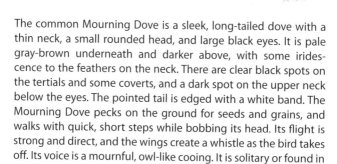

The common Mourning Dove is a sleek, long-tailed dove with a thin neck, a small rounded head, and large black eyes. It is pale gray-brown underneath and darker above, with some iridescence to the feathers on the neck. There are clear black spots on the tertials and some coverts, and a dark spot on the upper neck below the eyes. The pointed tail is edged with a white band. The Mourning Dove pecks on the ground for seeds and grains, and walks with quick, short steps while bobbing its head. Its flight is strong and direct, and the wings create a whistle as the bird takes off. Its voice is a mournful, owl-like cooing. It is solitary or found in small groups, but may form large flocks where food is abundant. The adult is illustrated.

Rock Pigeon, *Columba livia*
Family Columbidae (Pigeons, Doves)
Size: 12"
Season: Year-round
Habitat: Urban areas, farmland

The Rock Pigeon is the common pigeon seen in almost every urban area across the continent. Introduced from Europe, where they inhabit rocky cliffs, Rock Doves have adapted to city life, and domestication has resulted in a wide variety of plumage colors and patterns. The original, wild version is a stocky gray bird with a darker head and neck, and green to purple iridescence along the sides of the neck. The eyes are bright red, and the bill has a fleshy white cere on the base of the upper mandible. There are two dark bars across the back when the wing is folded, the rump is white, and the tail has a dark terminal band. Variants range from white to brown to black, with many pattern combinations. The adult is illustrated.

White-winged Dove,
Zenaida asiatica
Family Columbidae (Pigeons, Doves)
Size: 11.5"
Season: Year-round
Habitat: Open woodlands, desert scrub, urban and agricultural areas

The White-winged Dove is similar in shape to the Mourning Dove but is heavier with a shorter tail and broader wings. It is brownish-gray overall with dark wing tips and a broad white patch along the upper wing coverts that forms a white arc on the outer edges of the folded wing. The fanned tail shows white outer corners. There is a blue orbital ring around the brownish eyes, and a black spot along the lower cheek. White-winged Doves forage for seeds, fruits, or cacti. The voice is an owl-like, mournful *whoo-whoo-ca-whoo*. Their range, once limited to far southern Texas, is expanding across the state as the bird adapts to most habitats, including urban areas. The adult is illustrated.

Inca Dove, *Columbina inca*
Family Columbidae (Pigeons, Doves)
Size: 8.25"
Season: Year-round
Habitat: Dry, open woodlands; urban and agricultural areas

The Inca Dove is a small, squat, terrestrial bird with a long tail and short legs. It is pale, peachy-gray overall with a distinctive scaled appearance due to the dark outer margins of its feathers. The outer tail feathers are white. The short, rounded wings are rufous-brown tipped with black. This wing coloring is concealed in the folded wing but evident during flight or when it curiously lifts an extended wing skyward while on the ground. Juveniles are pale gray-brown overall with no dark scaling. Inca Doves forage on the ground for seeds, and their call is a repetitive, two-part cooing. The adult is illustrated.

Yellow-billed Cuckoo,
Coccyzus americanus
Family Cuculidae (Cuckoos)
Size: 12"
Season: Summer
Habitat: Woodlands, streamsides, swamps

Like the other cuckoos, the Yellow-billed Cuckoo is secretive and shy, hiding in vegetation, where it picks insects, caterpillars, and fruit from trees. It is brown above with rufous flight feathers and crisp white below. The bill is yellow with black along the top ridge. The tail is long and gradated with large white spots on the underside. The illustration shows an adult. It picks insects, caterpillars, and fruits from the tree canopy, and voices a quick, tapping *kak-kak-kak* or a series of throaty *coo* notes.

Greater Roadrunner,
Geococcyx californianus
Family Cuculidae (Cuckoos)
Size: 23"
Season: Year-round
Habitat: Open fields, grasslands, urban areas

The Greater Roadrunner is a very large ground-dwelling cuckoo with rounded wings, a long tail, a long neck, and a strong, pointed bill. It is heavily streaked overall, except for its pale gray belly. A pale blue patch appears behind the eyes, and its short, shaggy crest is often raised. The legs are long and sturdy. Roadrunners run with their tail held horizontal and their neck outstretched, and rarely fly. They forage by chasing down reptiles, insects, and rodents. Call is a deep cooing. The adult is illustrated.

Barn Owl, *Tyto alba*
Family Tytonidae (Barn Owls)
Size: 23"
Season: Year-round
Habitat: Barns, farmland, open areas with mature trees

The Barn Owl is a large-headed pale owl with small dark eyes, a heart-shaped facial disk, and long feathered legs. The wings, back, tail, and crown are light rusty brown with light gray smudging and small white dots. The underside, face, and underwing linings are white, with spots of rust on the breast. Females are usually darker than males, with more color and spotting across the breast and sides. The facial disk is enclosed by a thin line of darker feathers. Barn Owls are nocturnal hunters for rodents, and their call is a haunting, raspy *screeee!* The adult male is illustrated.

Great Horned Owl,
Bubo virginianus
Family Strigidae (Typical Owls)
Size: 22"
Season: Year-round
Habitat: Almost any environment, from forests to plains to urban areas

Found throughout North America, the Great Horned Owl is a large, strong owl with an obvious facial disk and long, sharp talons. Plumage is variable: Pacific and eastern forms are brown overall with heavy barring, a brown face, and a white chin patch, while southwestern forms are grayer and paler. The prominent ear tufts give the owl its name, and the eyes are large and yellow. The Great Horned Owl has exceptional hearing and sight. It feeds at night, perching on branches or posts and then swooping down on silent wings to catch birds, snakes, or mammals up to the size of a cat. Voice is a low *hoo-hoo-hoo*. The adult is illustrated.

Burrowing Owl,
Athene cunicularia
Family Strigidae (Typical Owls)
Size: 9.5"
Season: Year-round in western Texas
Habitat: Open grasslands and plains

The Burrowing Owl is a ground-dwelling owl that lives in burrows that have been vacated by ground squirrels and other rodents. It is small and flat headed, and has a short tail and long legs. Plumage is brown spotted with white above, and extensively barred brown and white below. It has a white chin and throat and bright yellow eyes. Burrowing Owls can be seen day or night perched on the ground or on a post, scanning for insects and small rodents. They sometimes exhibit a bowing movement when approached. Voice is a chattering or cooing, and sometimes imitative of a rattlesnake. The adult is illustrated.

Eastern Screech Owl,
Megascops asio
Family Strigidae (Typical Owls)
Size: 8.5"
Season: Year-round
Habitat: Wooded areas or parks, places where cavity-bearing trees exist

The Eastern Screech Owl is a small, but big-headed, eared owl with a short tail and bright yellow eyes. The highly camouflaged plumage ranges from brown to gray, depending on region. It is darker above, and streaked and barred below. The ear tufts may be drawn back to give the appearance of a rounded head, and the bill is grayish green tipped with white. White spots on the margins of the coverts and scapulars create two white bars on the folded wing. It is a nocturnal bird, hunting during the night for small mammals, insects, or fish. Its voice is a descending whistling call or a rapid staccato of one pitch. The adult is illustrated.

Barred Owl, *Strix varia*
Family Strigidae (Typical Owls)
Size: 21"
Season: Year-round
Habitat: Wooded swamps, upland forests

The Barred Owl is a large, compact owl with a short tail and wings, rounded head, and big, dark eyes. It lacks the ear tufts seen on the Great Horned Owl and has comparatively small talons. Plumage is gray-brown overall with dark barring on the neck and breast, turning to streaking on the belly and flanks. It swoops from its perch to catch small rodents, frogs, or snakes. Its voice, often heard during the day, is a hooting, *who-cooks-for-you,* or a kind of bark. Its nests are made in tree cavities vacated by other species. The illustration shows an adult.

Common Poorwill, *Phalaenoptilus nuttallii*

Family Caprimulgidae (Nightjars, Nighthawks)

Size: 8"

Season: Year-round in southwest Texas, summer only in northwest Texas

Habitat: Arid plains and shrubland, rocky areas

The Common Poorwill is a very small nightjar with an oversize head, rounded wings, and a very short, stubby tail. Plumage is cryptically mottled and barred grayish overall, with a white chin stripe and darker areas around the eyes and upper breast. The outer edges of the tail are white, and the wings are brown with dark barring. The tiny bill is based with heavy whiskers. From a ground perch, Common Poorwills flutter up to catch insects in flight. They are mostly nocturnal and ground dwelling, and may even hibernate during winter months. The adult is illustrated.

Common Nighthawk,

Chordeiles minor

Family Caprimulgidae (Nightjars, Nighthawks)

Size: 9"

Season: Summer

Habitat: Forests, marshes, plains, urban areas

The Common Nighthawk is primarily nocturnal, but may often be seen flying during the day and evening hours, catching insects on the wing with bounding flight. It is cryptically mottled gray, brown, and black, with strong barring on an otherwise pale underside. In the male, a white breast band is evident. The tail is long and slightly notched, and the wings are long and pointed, extending past the tail in the perched bird. In flight there is a distinct white patch on both sides of the wings. During the day, it is usually seen roosting on posts or branches with its eyes closed. Its voice is a short, nasal, buzzing sound. The illustration shows an adult male.

Chimney Swift,
Chaetura Pelagica
Family Apodidae (Swifts)
Size: 5"
Season: Summer
Habitat: Woods, scrub, swamps, urban areas

The gregarious Chimney Swift is unrelated to the swallows but similar in shape. The body is like a fat torpedo with a very short tail and long, pointed, bowed wings that bend close to the body. It is dark brown overall and slightly paler underneath and at the chin. Constantly on the wing, it catches insects in flight with quick wing beats and fast glides. It never perches, but roosts at night on vertical cliffs, trees, or in chimneys. Voice is a quick chattering uttered in flight. The adult is illustrated.

Black-chinned Hummingbird,
Archilochus alexandri
Family Trochilidae (Hummingbirds)
Size: 3.5"
Season: Summer
Habitat: Riparian areas in woodlands, canyons, areas with oak trees

The Black-chinned Hummingbird is a small, delicate bird able to hover on wings that beat at a blinding speed. The long, needle-like bill is used to probe deep into flowers so the bird can lap up nectar. The body is white below and green above, and the feet are tiny. Males have a dark green crown and iridescent violet-and-black throat, or gorget. Females lack the colored gorget and have a light green crown and white-tipped tail feathers. Its behavior is typical of hummingbirds, hovering and buzzing from flower to flower, emitting chits and squeaks. Most of these birds migrate across the Gulf of Mexico to South America in the winter. The female (top) and male (bottom) are illustrated.

Rufous Hummingbird,
Selasphorus rufus
Family Trochilidae (Hummingbirds)
Size: 3.5"
Season: Winter in eastern Texas, migrant elsewhere
Habitat: Woodlands, parks, gardens

The Rufous Hummingbird is a small, compact hummingbird with a relatively short bill and short wings. The male is bright rufous orange, with green wings, a white breast patch, and an iridescent bronze gorget (throat patch). The tail is tipped with black. Females have white tips on the outer tail feathers, a green back and crown, and a whitish chin with rufous spotting that sometimes forms a congealed spot in the middle. Rufous Hummingbirds drink nectar from flowers and feeders, and sometimes eat small insects. The female (top) and male (bottom) are illustrated.

Ruby-throated Hummingbird,
Archilochus colubris
Family Trochilidae (Hummingbirds)
Size: 3.5"
Season: Summer
Habitat: Areas with flowering plants, gardens, urban feeders

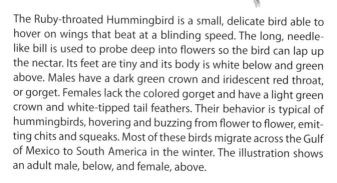

The Ruby-throated Hummingbird is a small, delicate bird able to hover on wings that beat at a blinding speed. The long, needle-like bill is used to probe deep into flowers so the bird can lap up the nectar. Its feet are tiny and its body is white below and green above. Males have a dark green crown and iridescent red throat, or gorget. Females lack the colored gorget and have a light green crown and white-tipped tail feathers. Their behavior is typical of hummingbirds, hovering and buzzing from flower to flower, emitting chits and squeaks. Most of these birds migrate across the Gulf of Mexico to South America in the winter. The illustration shows an adult male, below, and female, above.

Belted Kingfisher,
Megaceryle alcyon
Family Alcedinidae (Kingfishers)
Size: 13"
Season: Year-round
Habitat: Creeks, lakes, sheltered coastline

The widespread but solitary Belted Kingfisher is a stocky, large-headed bird with a powerful long bill and shaggy crest. It is grayish blue-green above and white below, with a thick blue band across the breast and white dotting on the back. White spots are at the lores. The female has an extra breast band of rufous, and is rufous along the flanks. Belted Kingfishers feed by springing from a perch along the water's edge or by hovering above the water and then plunging headfirst to snatch fish, frogs, or tadpoles. Its flight is uneven, and its voice is a raspy, rattling sound. The adult female is illustrated.

Green Kingfisher,
Chloroceryle americana
Family Alcedinidae (Kingfishers)
Size: 8.75"
Season: Year-round
Habitat: Small streams, lakesides with bushy shores

The Green Kingfisher is a very small kingfisher with a relatively large head and a massive, daggerlike bill. It is emerald green above and on the head, with white spotting on the wings and tail, and a broad, white collar about the neck. It is white below with a rufous breast band (male) or double green breast bands (female). The forehead and top of the head is flat and meets with a crest on the hind crown. Green Kingfishers plunge-dive for small fish and amphibians from a perch or after coursing low over the water surface. The voice is a curious, two-part tapping sound, similar to rocks clinking together. They are quieter and more secretive than the larger Belted Kingfishers, and they often twitch or pump their tails. The adult male is illustrated.

Red-headed Woodpecker,
Melanerpes erythrocephalus
Family Picidae (Woodpeckers)
Size: 9"
Season: Year-round
Habitat: Woodlands, areas with standing dead trees, suburbs

The Red-headed Woodpecker has a striking bright red head and a powerful, tapered bill. It is black above with a large patch of white across the lower back and secondaries, and white below. The juvenile has a pale brown head and incomplete white back patch. In all woodpeckers the tail is very stiff with sharp tips to aid in support while clinging to a tree trunk. To feed, it pecks at bark for insects but may also fly out to snatch its prey in midair. Nuts will also be taken and stored in tree cavities for winter. This species has been losing nesting cavities since the introduction of the European Starling. The illustration shows an adult.

Golden-fronted Woodpecker,
Melanerpes aurifrons
Family Picidae (Woodpeckers)
Size: 9.5"
Season: Year-round
Habitat: Dry, open woods or brushlands

A Texas specialty, the Golden-fronted Woodpecker is structurally similar to the Red-bellied Woodpecker of eastern states, and the Gila Woodpecker to the west. It is barred black-and-white along the back and wings with a black tail and a white rump. Below, it is pale brown and washed with yellow on the belly, with dark spotting at the vent. There are bright golden-yellow patches at the forehead and nape, with an additional red crown patch on the males. They pick insects from bark or by flycatching, and will also eat nuts and fruit. The voice consists of raucous, raspy chattering notes and a slurred *churr*. The illustration shows an adult male.

Downy Woodpecker,

Picoides pubescens
Family Picidae (Woodpeckers)
Size: 6.5"
Season: Year-round
Habitat: Woodlands, parks in urban areas,
streamsides

The Downy Woodpecker is a tiny woodpecker with a small bill and a relatively large head. It is white underneath with no barring, has black wings barred with white, and has a patch of white on the back. The head is boldly patterned black and white, and the male sports a red nape patch. The base of the bill joins the head with fluffy nasal tufts. Juveniles may show some red on the forehead and crown. Downy Woodpeckers forage for berries and insects in the bark and among the smaller twigs of trees. The very similar Hairy Woodpecker is larger, with a longer bill and more aggressive foraging behavior, sticking to larger branches and not clinging to twigs. The adult male is illustrated.

Northern Flicker,

Colaptes auratus
Family Picidae (Woodpeckers)
Size: 12.5"
Season: Year-round
Habitat: Variety of habitats, including
suburbs and parks

The common Northern Flicker is a large, long-tailed woodpecker often seen foraging on the ground for ants and other small insects. It is barred brown and black across the back, and buff with black spotting below. The head is brown, with a gray nape and crown. On the upper breast is a prominent half-circle of black, and the male has a red patch at the malar region. Flight is undulating and shows an orange wing lining and white rump. Its voice is a loud, sharp *keee,* and it will sometimes drum its bill repeatedly at objects, like a jackhammer. The Northern Flicker is sometimes referred to as the Red-shafted Flicker. The male is illustrated.

Pileated Woodpecker,
Dryocopus pileatus
Family Picidae (Woodpeckers)
Size: 16.5"
Season: Year-round
Habitat: Old-growth forests, urban areas with large trees

The Pileated Woodpecker is the largest woodpecker, except for the huge, probably extinct Ivory-billed Woodpecker. It is powerful, long necked, and crested. The body is all black, with a white base to the primaries, which are mostly covered in the folded wing. The head is boldly patterned black and white, with a bright red crest that is limited on the female. The male has a red malar patch, while that of the female is black. In flight, the contrasting white wing lining can be seen. To forage, Pileated Woodpeckers chip away chunks of bark to uncover ants and beetles, but will feed on berries during the winter months. Their voice is a high-pitched, uneven, resounding *wok-wok-wok*. The adult male is illustrated.

PASSERINES

Willow Flycatcher,
Empidonax traillii
Family Tyrannidae (Tyrant Flycatchers)
Size: 5.75"
Season: Transient migrant
Habitat: Moist, brushy areas with willows; foothill fields

The Willow Flycatcher is similar to many flycatchers in the genus Empidonax. It has a crown that peaks at the rear of the head and a fairly thick bill. Plumage is greenish brown-gray above with pale, dusky underparts and a whitish chin and throat. A thin white eye-ring is around the eyes, the lores are light, and the lower mandible is pale orange. Distinct wing bars are visible on the folded wing. Willow Flycatchers catch insects, starting from a perch and then returning to the same spot. Their voice is a high, nasal *fitz-bee* call. The adult is illustrated.

Black Phoebe, *Sayornis nigricans*
Family Tyrannidae (Tyrant Flycatchers)
Size: 7"
Season: Year-round in eastern Texas
Habitat: Open woodlands, gardens, shrubs—usually near water

The Black Phoebe is a long-tailed flycatcher with a relatively big head and a short, thin, pointed bill. Plumage is sooty black above, on the head, and on the breast and sides. It is white underneath, coming to a point at the breast. The crown is often peaked, and the outer tail feathers show a thin white stripe. Black Phoebes perch upright and bob their tails up and down, and they voice a high-pitched, whistled *seep*. They flycatch for insects from a low perch, and are often seen hovering. The adult is illustrated.

Say's Phoebe, *Sayornis saya*
Family Tyrannidae (Tyrant Flycatchers)
Size: 7.5"
Season: Year-round in western Texas, summer in southern Texas
Habitat: Arid, open country, shrubland

The Say's Phoebe is a fairly slim flycatcher with a long, black tail. It is pale gray brown above, with lighter wing bars. The underside is whitish to gray under the chin and breast, fading to orange brown on the belly and undertail coverts. The head has a flat crown that often peaks toward the rear, and the bird has dark eyes, lores, and bill. It flycatches for insects from a perch on rocks or twigs. The Say's Phoebe voices a high, whistled *pit-eur,* and often pumps or flares out its tail. The adult is illustrated.

Vermillion Flycatcher,
Procephalus rubinus
Family Tyrannidae (Tyrant Flycatchers)
Size: 6"
Season: Year-round in southern Texas
Habitat: Open brushlands or woodlands, usually near water

The unmistakable Vermillion Flycatcher is a small but large-headed flycatcher with a short, thin bill. The sexes are dramatically different in plumage. Males are dark gray-brown on the back, tail, and wings, and vermillion red below and on the head. There is a dark stripe running through the eyes and the red crown is often raised. The female is pale brown above and white below, with gray streaking on the breast and a pinkish-buff wash on the lower belly and undertail coverts. The face is white with a brown auricular patch and crown. Vermillion Flycatchers spring from a low perch to flycatch for insects, and voice a high-pitched, accelerating series of quick *chips,* ending in a short trill. The male (left) and female (right) are illustrated.

Great Kiskadee, *Pitangus sulfuratus*
Family Tyrannidae (Tyrant Flycatchers)
Size: 9.75"
Season: Year-round in far southern Texas
Habitat: Woodlands and thickets
near water

Although fairly common in southern Texas, this is the only place to find the Great Kiskadee in the United States. It is a stocky, distinctively marked flycatcher with a large head and stout bill. It is brown above with rufous edges to the wings and tail feathers, and bright yellow below. The head is white with a black crown and stripe across the face. A thin, yellow median crown patch can be seen when the fore-crown is raised. Kiskadees are opportunistic feeders, taking small vertebrates, insects, fruit, or fish. The voice consists of loud squawks and a higher pitched *kis-ka-dee*. The adult is illustrated.

Eastern Kingbird,
Tyrannus tyrannus
Family Tyrannidae (Tyrant Flycatchers)
Size: 8.5"
Season: Summer
Habitat: Open woodlands, agricultural and rural areas

The Eastern Kingbird is a slender, medium-size flycatcher. Its upperparts are bluish black, and its underparts are white with a pale gray breast. The dark head cap contrasts with the white lower half of the face. The tail is black with a white terminal band. It flies with shallow wing beats on wings that are mostly dark and pointed. Eastern Kingbirds perch on wires, treetops, or posts and take flight to capture insects on the wing. The voice is a distinctive series of very high-pitched, sputtering, zippy *psit* notes. The adult is illustrated.

Western Kingbird,
Tyrannus verticalis
Family Tyrannidae (Tyrant Flycatchers)
Size: 8.75"
Season: Summer
Habitat: Open fields, agricultural areas

The Western Kingbird is a relatively slender flycatcher with a stout black bill and a slightly rounded black tail with white along the outer edge. It is grayish- or greenish-brown above, pale gray on the breast, and bright yellow on the belly, sides, and under-tail coverts. The head is light gray, with a white throat and malar area, and dark gray at the lores and behind the eyes. There is a small reddish crown patch that is normally concealed. Western Kingbirds flycatch for insects from a perch on branches, posts, or wires, and their voice is composed of quick, high-pitched *zips* and *chits*. The adult is illustrated.

Scissor-tailed Flycatcher,
Tyrannus forficatus
Family Tyrannidae
(Tyrant Flycatchers)
Size: 8.75"
Season: Summer
Habitat: Open fields,
agricultural areas

The Scissor-tailed Flycatcher is aptly named with its incredibly long, forked tail. It has dark wings, a gray back, and pale gray underparts. The head is pale gray with black eyes and bill. It has rusty pink on the belly and undertail coverts. Females and juveniles have a shorter tail and are paler overall. In flight one can see the rusty-pink wing linings. It flycatches for insects, but also eats seeds and berries when they are available. The illustration shows an adult male.

Loggerhead Shrike,
Lanius ludovicianus
Family Laniidae (Shrikes)
Size: 9.5"
Season: Year-round
Habitat: Dry open country

The solitary Loggerhead Shrike is raptor-like in its feeding habits. It swoops down from its perch on a branch, wire, or post and captures large insects, small mammals, or birds, impaling them on thorny barbs before tearing them apart to feed. It is a compact, large-headed bird with a short, thick, slightly hooked bill. The upperparts are gray, and the underparts are pale. The wings are black, with white patches at the base of the primaries and upper coverts. The tail is black and edged with white. There is a black mask on the head extending from the base of the bill to the ear areas. Juveniles show a finely barred breast. Flight is composed of quick wing beats and swooping glides. The adult is illustrated.

White-eyed Vireo, *Vireo griseus*
Family Vireonidae (Vireos)
Size: 5"
Season: Year-round near the
Gulf Coast, summer inland
Habitat: Dense woodlands,
thickets, shrubs

The White-eyed Vireo is a small, chunky vireo with a relatively large head and short bill. It is grayish olive-green above and pale gray below, tinged with yellow on the flanks and undertail coverts. The head is grayish with conspicuous, yellow "spectacles," or combined lores and eye-ring areas. The large eyes are white. On the wings are two white wing bars. The juvenile bird has darker eyes than that of the adult. This bird gleans insects, spiders, and berries from the dense vegetation. The illustration shows an adult.

Red-eyed Vireo,
Vireo olivaceus
Family Vireonidae (Vireos)
Size: 6"
Season: Summer
Habitat: Areas of dense vegetation, mature deciduous forests

The Red-eyed Vireo is a sluggish, slow-moving bird that haunts the upper tree canopy picking out insects and berries. Its head appears rather flat and its tail is short. It is light olive-green above and white below with a yellow wash across the breast, flanks, and undertail coverts. It has dark eye-lines, white eye-brows, and a grayish crown. The eyes are red and the bill is fairly large with a hooked tip. Its voice is a repetitive, incessant song in single phrases. The illustration shows an adult.

Green Jay, *Cyanocorax yncas*
Family Corvidae (Jays, Crows)
Size: 10.5"
Season: Year-round
Habitat: Open woodlands, dense thickets, urban parks

The Green Jay is an unmistakable, brilliantly plumaged jay with a long tail and short bill. The body is green above, paler green below, with yellow underwing linings, tail edges, and undertail coverts. The head is blue with black patterning around the eyes, and the breast and throat are black. Green Jays forage for seeds, fruit, and insects, and commonly visit feeders. The voice is a series of short, raspy notes. A Texas specialty, it is found only in southern Texas and Central America. The adult is illustrated.

Blue Jay, *Cyanocitta cristata*
Family Corvidae (Jays, Crows)
Size: 11"
Season: Year-round
Habitat: Woodlands, rural and urban areas

The solitary Blue Jay is a sturdy, crested jay. It is bright blue above and white below with a thick, tapered, black bill. There is a white patch around the eyes to the chin, bordered by a thin, black "necklace" extending to the back of the nape. It has a conspicuous white wing bar and dark barring on wings and tail. In flight the white outer edges of the tail are visible as it alternates shallow wing beats with glides. Omnivorous, the Blue Jay eats just about anything, especially acorns, nuts, fruits, insects, and small vertebrates. It is a raucous and noisy bird and quite bold. Sometimes it mimics the calls of birds of prey. The illustration shows an adult.

JAYS, CROWS

Western Scrub-Jay,
Aphelocoma californica
Family Corvidae (Jays, Crows)
Size: 11.5"
Season: Year-round
Habitat: Open scrub-oak, urban areas

The Western Scrub-Jay is a long-necked, sleek, crestless jay. The upperparts are deep blue, with a distinct, lighter gray-brown mantle. The underparts are pale gray, becoming white on the belly and undertail coverts. It has a thin white superciliary stripe, the malar area is dark gray, and the throat is streaked with white and gray above a pale, gray-blue "necklace" across the breast. Flight is an undulating combination of rapid wing beats and swooping glides. Its diet consists of nuts, seeds, insects, and fruit. The adult is illustrated.

American Crow,
Corvus brachyrhynchus
Family Corvidae (Jays, Crows)
Size: 17.5"
Season: Year-round
Habitat: Open woodlands, pastures, rural fields, dumps

The American Crow is a widespread corvid found across the continent, voicing its familiar, loud, grating *caw-caw*. It is a large, stocky bird with a short, rounded tail, broad wings, and a thick, powerful bill. Plumage is glistening black overall in all stages of development. It will eat almost anything, and often forms loose flocks with other crows. The adult is illustrated.

Purple Martin, *Progne subis*
Family Hirundinidae (Swallows)
Size: 8"
Season: Summer
Habitat: Marshes, open water, agricultural areas

The Purple Martin is the largest North American swallow. It has long, pointed wings, a streamlined body, and a forked tail. The bill is very short and broad at the base. The male is dark overall, with a blackish-blue sheen across the back and head, while the female is paler overall, with sooty, mottled underparts. Flight consists of fast wing beats alternating with circular glides. Purple Martins commonly use man-made nest boxes or tree hollows as nesting sites. The male is illustrated.

Northern Rough-winged Swallow,
Stelgidopteryx serripennis
Family Hirundinidae (Swallows)
Size: 5.5"
Season: Year-round in far southern Texas, summer elsewhere
Habitat: Sandy cliffs, steep streamsides, outcrops, bridges

The Northern Rough-winged Swallow flies in a smooth and even fashion, with full wing beats, feeding on insects caught on the wing. It is uniform brownish above and white below. The breast is lightly streaked with pale brown, and the tail is short and square. Juveniles show light rust-colored wing bars on the upper coverts. These fairly solitary swallows find nesting sites in holes in sandy cliffs. The adult is illustrated.

Tree Swallow, *Tachycineta bicolor*
Family Hirundinidae (Swallows)
Size: 5.75"
Season: Fall and spring transient
Habitat: Variety of habitats near water and perching sites

The Tree Swallow has a short, slightly notched tail, broad-based triangular wings, and a thick neck. It has a high-contrast plumage pattern, with dark metallic green-blue upperparts and crisp white underparts. When perched, the primaries reach just past the tail tip. Juveniles are gray-brown below, with a subtle, darker breast band. Tree Swallows take insects on the wing, but will also eat berries and fruits. They often form huge lines of individuals perched on wires or branches. The Tree Swallow's voice is a high-pitched chirping. The male is illustrated.

Barn Swallow, *Hirundo rustica*
Family Hirundinidae (Swallows)
Size: 6.5"
Season: Summer
Habitat: Old buildings, caves, open rural areas near bridges

The widespread and common Barn Swallow has narrow, pointed wings and a long, deeply forked tail. It is pale below and dark blue above, with a rusty-orange forehead and throat. The male's underparts are pale orange, while the female's are pale cream. Barn Swallows are graceful, fluid fliers, and they often forage in groups to catch insects in flight. They build cup-shaped nests of mud on almost any protected man-made structure. Voice is a loud, repetitive chirping or clicking. The adult male is illustrated.

Carolina Chickadee,
Poecile carolinensis
Family Paridae (Chickadees, Titmice)
Size: 4.75"
Season: Year-round
Habitat: Woodlands, feeders

The Carolina Chickadee is a small, compact, active bird with short, rounded wings. It is gray above and lighter gray or dusky below with a contrasting black cap and throat patch. It is quite similar to the Black-capped Chickadee, which does not normally occur in Texas. Its voice sounds like the name, *chick-a-dee, dee, dee,* or a soft *fee-bay.* It is quite social and feeds on a variety of seeds, berries, and insects found in trees and shrubs. The illustration shows an adult.

Verdin, *Auriparus flaviceps*
Family Remizidae (Verdins)
Size: 4.5"
Season: Year-round
Habitat: Low elevation desert
scrublands

The Verdin is a solitary, small bird with a small, sharp bill and chickadee-like habits. It is gray overall, paler below, with a golden-yellow head and a small, rufous shoulder patch. Sexes are similar, but the females have less yellow on the head and are duller over-all. Juveniles are entirely gray. Verdins actively flit among thorny thickets, foraging for insects. The voice is a clear, high-pitched, whistled *tew*. The male is illustrated.

Bushtit, *Psaltriparus minimus*
Family Aegithalidae (Bushtits)
Size: 4.5"
Season: Year-round
Habitat: Mixed woodlands,
scrubland, oaks

The Bushtit is a tiny, ball-shaped, fluffy bird with short, rounded wings and a long tail. Its drab plumage is brownish-gray above and paler gray underneath. The eyes of the female are light yel-low, while those of the male are black. The bill is short and stubby, with a curved culmen, and the legs are thin and dark. Bushtits flit from tree to tree in noisy groups, eating berries and insects. Their voice is a thin, high-pitched, rapid series of twittering *chips*. The adult female is illustrated.

White-breasted Nuthatch,

Sitta carolinensis
Family Sittidae (Nuthatches)
Size: 5.75"
Season: Year-round in northeastern Texas
Habitat: Mixed oak and coniferous woodlands

The White-breasted Nuthatch has a large head and wide neck, short rounded wings, and a short tail. It is blue-gray above and pale gray below, with rusty smudging on the lower flanks and undertail coverts. The breast and face are white, and there is a black crown merging with the mantle. The bill is long, thin, and upturned at the tip. To forage, it creeps headfirst down tree trunks to pick out insects and seeds. It nests in tree cavities high off the ground. Its voice is a nasal, repetitive *auk-auk-auk*. The adult male is illustrated.

Rock Wren, *Salpinctes obsoletus*
Family Troglodytidae (Wrens)
Size: 6"
Season: Year-round
Habitat: Open, dry, rocky areas; deserts

The Rock Wren is a stocky bird with a short tail, a large head, and a thin, slightly downcurved bill. It is grayish-brown above, with fine barring and spotting. Underneath it is pale buff to gray, with fine streaking along the breast and dark bars on the undertail coverts. There is a pale superciliary stripe above the dark eyes. The pale brownish tips of the outer tail feathers can be seen when the tail is fanned. Rock Wrens search around rocks for insects, flitting from rock to rock and often bobbing up and down. The adult is illustrated.

Canyon Wren,

Catherpes mexicanus
Family Troglodytidae (Wrens)
Size: 5.75"
Season: Year-round in western Texas
Habitat: Rocky cliffs and canyons, rocky streamsides

The Canyon Wren has a short tail, a flat head, and a long, slightly downcurved bill. It is rufous-brown with black barring and spotting on the back, tail, and underparts. The head is gray-brown above and white below the eyes, with a white throat and breast. Juveniles are patterned as adults but lack spotting on the back and belly. Canyon Wrens deftly scramble among rocks, reaching into tight crevices to pick out insects and spiders. The voice is a series of sweet, musical notes followed by dry, buzzy notes.

Carolina Wren,

Thryothorus ludovicianus
Family Troglodytidae (Wrens)
Size: 5.5"
Season: Year-round
Habitat: Understory of wooded and brushy areas, swamps

The Carolina Wren is a vocal but cryptic bird, usually hidden among dense foliage close to the ground. It lurks in vegetation picking out insects, seeds, or fruit, emitting a musical song or a harsh, quick call. The body is plump with a short, rounded tail and a thin, slightly downcurved bill. It is dark rusty-brown above, buffy below, and has a long, white superciliary stripe extending to the nape. Wings and tail are thinly barred with black. This bird habitually holds its tail in a cocked-up position. The illustration shows an adult.

Marsh Wren, *Cistothorus palustris*
Family Troglodytidae (Wrens)
Size: 5"
Season: Winter
Habitat: Marshes, reeds,
stream banks

The Marsh Wren is a small, cryptic, rufous-brown wren with a normally cocked-up tail. The tail and wings are barred with black, and the chin and breast are white. There is a well-defined white superciliary stripe below a uniform brown crown, and the mantle shows distinct black-and-white striping. The bill is long and slightly decurved. Marsh Wrens are vocal day and night with quick, repetitive cheeping. They are secretive but inquisitive, and glean insects from the marsh vegetation and water surface. The illustration shows an adult.

GNATCATCHERS

Blue-gray Gnatcatcher,
Polioptila caerulea
Family Polioptilidae (Gnatcatchers)
Size: 4.5"
Season: Year-round in southern Texas,
summer elsewhere
Habitat: Deciduous or pine woodlands, thickets

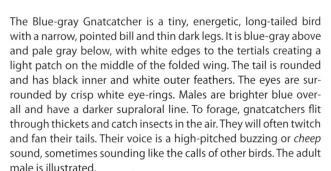

The Blue-gray Gnatcatcher is a tiny, energetic, long-tailed bird with a narrow, pointed bill and thin dark legs. It is blue-gray above and pale gray below, with white edges to the tertials creating a light patch on the middle of the folded wing. The tail is rounded and has black inner and white outer feathers. The eyes are surrounded by crisp white eye-rings. Males are brighter blue overall and have a darker supraloral line. To forage, gnatcatchers flit through thickets and catch insects in the air. They will often twitch and fan their tails. Their voice is a high-pitched buzzing or *cheep* sound, sometimes sounding like the calls of other birds. The adult male is illustrated.

Ruby-crowned Kinglet,

Regulus calendula
Family Regulidae (Kinglets)
Size: 4"
Season: Winter
Habitat: Mixed woodlands,
brushy areas

The Ruby-crowned Kinglet is a tiny, plump songbird with a short tail and a diminutive, thin bill. It has a habit of nervously twitching its wings as it actively flits through vegetation, gleaning small insects and larvae. It may also hover in search of food. Plumage is pale olive green above and paler below, with patterned wings and pale wing bars on the upper coverts. There are white eye-rings, or crescents around the eyes. The bright red crest of the male bird is faintly noticeable unless the crest is raised. Voice is a very high-pitched, whistling *seeee*. The adult is illustrated.

Eastern Bluebird, *Sialia sialis*
Family Turdidae (Thrushes)
Size: 7"
Season: Year-round
Habitat: Open woodlands, pastures,
fields

The Eastern Bluebird is a member of the thrush family that travels in small groups, feeding on a variety of insects, spiders, and berries, and singing a series of musical *chur-lee* notes. It is a stocky, short-tailed, and short-billed bird that often perches in an upright posture on wires and posts. The male is brilliant blue above and rusty-orange below with a white belly and undertail region. The orange extends to the nape making a subtle collar. The female is paler overall with a white throat and eye-rings. Juveniles are brownish-gray with extensive white spotting and barred underparts. Man-made nest boxes have helped this species increase in numbers throughout its range. The illustration shows an adult male, below, and female, above.

American Robin,
Turdus migratorius
Family Turdidae (Thrushes)
Size: 10"
Season: Year-round
Habitat: Widespread in a variety of habitats, including woodlands, fields, parks, and lawns

Familiar and friendly, the American Robin is a large thrush with a long tail and long legs. It commonly holds its head cocked and keeps its wing tips lowered beneath its tail. It is gray-brown above and rufous below, with a darker head and contrasting white eye crescents and loral patches. The chin is streaked black and white, and the bill is yellow with darker edges. Females are typically paler overall, and juveniles show white spots above and dark spots below. Robins forage on the ground, picking out earthworms and insects, or in trees for berries. Song is a series of high, musical phrases, sounding like *cheery, cheer-u-up, cheerio.* The adult male is illustrated.

Hermit Thrush, *Catharus guttatus*
Family Turdidae (Thrushes)
Size: 7"
Season: Winter
Habitat: Woodlands, brushy areas

The Hermit Thrush is a compact, short-tailed thrush that habitually cocks its tail. It forages on the ground near vegetative cover for insects, worms, and berries, and voices a song of beautiful, flutelike notes. It is reddish to olive-brown above, with a rufous tail. The underparts are white, with dusky flanks and sides and black spotting on the throat and breast. The dark eyes are encircled by complete white eye-rings. In flight, the pale wing lining contrasts with the dark flight feathers. The adult is illustrated.

Northern Mockingbird,
Mimus polyglottos
Family Mimidae (Mockingbirds, Catbirds, Thrashers)
Size: 10.5"
Season: Year-round
Habitat: Open fields, grassy areas near vegetative cover, suburbs, parks

The state bird of Texas, the Northern Mockingbird is constantly vocalizing. Its scientific name, *polyglottos*, means "many voices," alluding to its amazing mimicry of the songs of other birds. It is sleek, long tailed, and long legged. Plumage is gray above, with darker wings and tail, and off-white to brownish-gray below. It has two white wing bars, short dark eye-stripes, and pale eye-rings. In flight, conspicuous white patches on the inner primaries and coverts and white outer tail feathers can be seen. Like other mimids, it forages on the ground for insects and berries, intermittently flicking its wings. The adult is illustrated.

Gray Catbird, *Dumetella carolinensis*
Family Mimidae (Mockingbirds, Catbirds, Thrashers)
Size: 8.5"
Season: Winter along the Gulf Coast, summer in eastern Texas
Habitat: Understory of woodland edges, shrubs, rural gardens

The solitary Gray Catbird is long necked and sleek with a sturdy, pointed bill. It is uniformly gray except for its rufous undertail coverts, black crown, and black, rounded tail. It is quite secretive and spends most of its time hidden in thickets close to the ground, picking through the substrate for insects, berries, and seeds. Its call includes a nasal, cat-like *meew* from which its name is derived, although it will also mimic the songs of other birds. To escape danger, it will often choose to run away rather than fly. The illustration shows an adult.

Brown Thrasher, *Toxostoma rufum*

Family Mimidae (Mockingbirds,
Catbirds, Thrashers)
Size: 11"
Season: Year-round in eastern Texas,
winter elsewhere
Habitat: Woodlands, thickets,
urban gardens, orchards

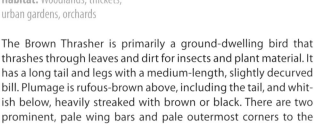

The Brown Thrasher is primarily a ground-dwelling bird that thrashes through leaves and dirt for insects and plant material. It has a long tail and legs with a medium-length, slightly decurved bill. Plumage is rufous-brown above, including the tail, and whitish below, heavily streaked with brown or black. There are two prominent, pale wing bars and pale outermost corners to the tail. Its eyes are yellow to orange. Its voice is a variety of musical phrases, often sung from a conspicuous perch. The illustration shows an adult.

Curve-billed Thrasher,

Toxostoma curvirostre
Family Mimidae (Mockingbirds, Catbirds,
Thrashers)
Size: 11"
Season: Year-round
Habitat: Dry brushlands, deserts,
urban areas

The Curve-billed Thrasher is a stocky, long-tailed, long-legged bird with a long, downcurved bill. It is overall gray-brown, paler below, with faint white wing bars and brownish spotting down the breast and belly. The eyes are bright orange, and the corners of the tail are white. They forage on the ground, probing the substrate and flicking away debris to find insects, seeds, and berries. The voice is a whistling, *wit-weet,* and a series of rapid, rambling, musical notes. The adult is illustrated.

European Starling, *Sturnus vulgaris*
Family Sturnidae (Starlings)
Size: 8.5"
Season: Year-round
Habitat: Found almost anywhere, particularly in rural fields, gardens, dumps, and urban parks

Introduced from Europe, the European Starling has successfully infiltrated most habitats in North America and competes with native birds for nest cavities. It is a stocky, sturdy, aggressive bird that is glossy black overall with a sheen of green or purple. The breeding adult has a yellow bill and greater iridescence, while the adult in winter is more flat black, with a black bill and numerous white spots. The tail is short and square. Starlings form very large, compact flocks, and fly directly on pointed, triangular wings. The diet of starlings is highly variable and includes insects, grains, and berries. Vocalizations include loud, wheezy whistles and clucks, and imitations of other birdsongs. The breeding adult is illustrated.

Cedar Waxwing,
Bombycilla cedrorum
Family Bombycillidae (Waxwings)
Size: 7"
Season: Winter
Habitat: Woodlands, swamps, urban areas near berry trees

The Cedar Waxwing is a compact, crested songbird with pointed wings and a short tail. The sleek, smooth plumage is brownish-gray overall, with paler underparts, a yellowish wash on the belly, and white undertail coverts. The head pattern is striking, with a crisp black mask thinly bordered by white. The tail is tipped with bright yellow, and the tips of the secondary feathers are coated with a unique red, waxy substance. Cedar Waxwings will form large flocks and devour berries from a tree, then move on to the next. They may also flycatch small insects. Their voice is an extremely high-pitched, whistling *seee*. The adult is illustrated.

Orange-crowned Warbler,
Oreothlypis celata
Family Parulidae (Wood-Warblers)
Size: 5"
Season: Winter
Habitat: Mixed woodlands, brushy thickets

The Orange-crowned Warbler is rather plain, with a relatively long tail and a thin, pointed bill. It is olive green above and brighter yellow below, streaked with olive, and the undertail coverts are solid yellow. It has short, dark eye-lines and thin, pale, broken eye-rings. There is much variation in this species, from brighter forms to grayer forms, and the orange crown patch is rarely visible. Orange-crowned Warblers forage for insects or berries in the undergrowth, and voice a long series of descending staccato *tit* notes. The adult is illustrated.

Northern Parula,
Parula americana
Family Parulidae (Wood-Warblers)
Size: 4.5"
Season: Summer in eastern Texas
Habitat: Treetops in mossy woodlands

The Northern Parula is a tiny, stubby warbler with a short, sharp bill, short tail, and a relatively large head. Upperparts are slatey blue with a greenish mantle. Below there is a white belly and undertail, a yellow chin and breast, and a rufous breast band. Above and below the eyes are white eye arcs, and the lower mandible is yellow. The wing shows two bold white wing bars. The female is bordered above the breast band with gray. Northern Parulas forage for insects and caterpillars in trees. The illustration shows an adult male.

Yellow Warbler,

Dendroica petechia
Family Parulidae (Wood-Warblers)
Size: 5"
Season: Fall and spring migrant
Habitat: Willows and alders near
streamsides, rural shrubbery, gardens

The Yellow Warbler is widespread in North America, and sings a musical *sweet-sweet-sweet*. It is bright yellow overall, with darker yellow-green above and reddish-brown streaking below. The black eyes stand out on its light face, and the bill is relatively thick for a warbler. Clean, yellow stripes are evident on the fanned tail. The female is paler overall, with less noticeable streaking on the breast and sides. Yellow Warblers forage in the brush for insects and spiders. The adult male is illustrated.

Yellow-rumped Warbler,

Dendroica coronata
Family Parulidae (Wood-Warblers)
Size: 5.5"
Season: Winter
Habitat: Deciduous and coniferous
woodlands, suburbs

Two races of this species occur in North America: The "myrtle" form ranges across the continent, and the "Audubon's" form can be found west of the Rockies and in eastern Texas. The "myrtle" variety is blue-gray above with dark streaks, and white below with black streaking below the chin and a bright yellow side patch. There is a black mask across the face, bordered by a thin superciliary stripe above and a white throat below. The nonbreeding adult and female are paler, with a more brownish cast to the upperparts. The longish tail has white spots on either side and meets with the conspicuous yellow rump. The "Audubon's" variety has a yellow chin and a gray face. Yellow-rumped Warblers prefer to eat berries and insects. The male "myrtle" form is illustrated.

Golden-cheeked Warbler,

Dendroica chrysoparia
Family Parulidae (Wood-Warblers)
Size: 5"
Season: Summer
Habitat: Juniper-oak woodlands
of central Texas

The rare and endangered Golden-cheeked Warbler is a true Texas specialty. It breeds only in Texas in areas including the Ashe Juniper and migrates to Central America during winter. It is dark gray above with white wing bars and outer tail feathers, and it is white below with broad, black streaks. On the large head is a golden-yellow face surrounded by black, and thin, black eye-lines. The female is paler overall with a yellow chin. The voice is a series of buzzy notes and melodic whistles. The adult male is illustrated.

American Redstart,

Setophaga ruticilla
Family Parulidae (Wood-Warblers)
Size: 5"
Season: Summer in eastern Texas,
migrant elsewhere
Habitat: Open mixed woodlands in
early succession

The constantly active, frenetic American Redstart often fans its tail and wings in display while perched. It is long tailed, and the plumages of males and females are markedly different. The male is jet black above, white below, with a fiery red patch at the side of the breast, and a paler, peachy-red wing bar and sides of the tail. The female is gray-green above with a slatey-gray head and white chin and breast. The colored areas are located in the same areas as on the male but are yellow. Redstarts eat insects gleaned from branches and bark, or flycatch for insects. The illustration shows an adult male, below, and female, above.

Prothonotary Warbler,
Protonotaria citrea
Family Parulidae (Wood-Warblers)
Size: 5.5"
Season: Summer
Habitat: Wooded swamps

Also known as the Golden Swamp Warbler, the Prothonotary Warbler is a fairly large warbler with a short tail, a relatively large head, and a long, sharp bill. The head and underparts are a rich yellow to yellow-orange, and the undertail coverts are white. The wings and tail are blue-gray and there is an olive-green mantle. Females and juveniles are paler overall with an olive cast to the head. Prothonotary Warblers forage through the understory for insects. The illustration shows an adult male.

Common Yellowthroat,
Geothlypis trichas
Family Parulidae (Wood-Warblers)
Size: 5"
Season: Year-round
Habitat: Low vegetation near water, swamps, fields

The Common Yellowthroat scampers through the undergrowth looking for insects and spiders in a somewhat wren-like manner. It is a plump little warbler that often cocks up its tail. Plumage is olive-brown above and pale brown to whitish below, with a bright yellow breast/chin region and undertail coverts. The male has a black facial mask trailed by a fuzzy white area on the nape. The female lacks the facial mask. The female (top) and male (bottom) are illustrated.

Hooded Warbler,
Wilsonia citrina
Family Parulidae (Wood-Warblers)
Size: 5"
Season: Summer
Habitat: Moist woodlands, swamps

The Hooded Warbler lurks in the woodland understory picking out insects while continually flicking its tail and singing its high, musical *weeta-weeta-weeta-toe*. Plumage is olive-green above and bright yellow below. The male has a full, black hood encompassing the face and chin, while the female has a fainter, partial mask with a yellow chin. In the fanned tail one can see white inner veins to the outer tail feathers. The illustration shows an adult male, below, and female, above.

WOOD-WARBLERS

Wilson's Warbler,
Wilsonia pusilla
Family Parulidae (Wood-Warblers)
Size: 4.75"
Season: Winter along the Gulf Coast, transient elsewhere
Habitat: Willow and alder thickets, woodlands near water

The Wilson's Warbler is a small, lively warbler with a narrow tail and a short bill. It is uniform olive green above and yellow below, with some olive-green smudging. The head has large black eyes and a beanie-shaped black cap. Females and juveniles have a greenish cap with variable amounts of black. Wilson's Warblers stay low to the ground, gleaning food from the vegetation, or hover and flycatch for insects. Their voice is a rapid series of chattering notes, or a quick *chip* call. The adult male is illustrated.

Yellow-breasted Chat,

Icteria virens
Family Parulidae (Wood-Warblers)
Size: 7.5"
Season: Summer
Habitat: Dense vegetation,
woodland edges

The largest wood-warbler, the Yellow-breasted Chat has a long, rounded tail and a heavy, pointed black bill with a strongly curved culmen. It is uniformly greenish-brown above. Below, the belly and undertail coverts are white, while the chin and breast are bright yellow. The head is dark, with bold white patterning above the lores, at the malar area, and around the eyes, forming white "spectacles." Females are slightly duller in color. Yellow-breasted Chats forage in low brush for insects and berries, and have quite variable vocalizations, including mimicking the songs of other birds. The male has a strange display behavior in which it hovers and dangles its legs. The adult is illustrated.

Spotted Towhee,

Pipilo maculatus
Family Emberizidae (Sparrows,
Buntings)
Size: 8.5"
Season: Winter
Habitat: Thickets, suburban shrubs,
gardens

The Spotted Towhee is a large, long-tailed sparrow with a thick, short bill and sturdy legs. It forages on the ground in dense cover by kicking back both feet at once to uncover insects, seeds, and worms. It is black above, including the head and upper breast, and has rufous sides and a white belly. It has white wing bars, white spotting on the scapulars and mantle, and white corners on the tail. The eye color is red. Females look like the males but are brown above. The Spotted Towhee and the Eastern Towhee were previously considered one species, the Rufous-sided Towhee. The adult male is illustrated.

Chipping Sparrow,

Spizella passerina
Family Emberizidae (Sparrows, Buntings)
Size: 5.5"
Season: Year-round
Habitat: Dry fields, woodland edges,
gardens

The Chipping Sparrow is a medium-size sparrow with a slightly notched tail and a rounded crest. It is barred black and brown on the upperparts, with a gray rump, and is pale gray below. The head has a rufous crown, white superciliary stripes, dark eye-lines, and white throat. The bill is short, conical, and pointed. The sexes are similar, and winter adults are duller and lack the rufous color on the crown. Chipping Sparrows feed in trees or on open ground in loose flocks, searching for seeds and insects. The voice is a rapid, staccato chipping sound. The breeding adult is illustrated.

Lark Sparrow,

Chondestes grammacus
Family Emberizidae (Sparrows,
Buntings)
Size: 6.5"
Season: Year-round
Habitat: Woodland edges, dry prairies
with brush, agricultural areas

The Lark Sparrow is an elongated, thin sparrow with a long, rounded tail. It is light brown above, streaked with dark brown, and white below with tan around the sides and flanks. There is a distinct dark spot in the middle of the breast. The head is patterned with a rufous crown that has a white medial stripe, rufous cheeks, black eye-lines, and black throat stripe. Lark Sparrows travel in small flocks, hopping or walking on the ground to pick up seeds and insects. They sing a variety of high-pitched chips and trills, often from a conspicuous perch. Males may display with their tails cocked up. The adult is illustrated.

Seaside Sparrow,
Ammodramus maritimus
Family Emberizidae (Sparrows, Buntings)
Size: 6"
Season: Year-round
Habitat: Coastal saltwater marshes, freshwater marshes

The Seaside Sparrow is plump with a relatively large, flat head, a fairly long bill, and a short tail. Plumage is olive-brown above with dark streaking, and white below with dark streaks or spots. The chin is white, bordered by an obvious moustachial stripe, and the supraloral region is yellow. This bird forages among the marsh vegetation for insects, seeds, and small crustaceans and snails. It dives quickly into cover from flight. The illustration shows an adult.

White-crowned Sparrow,
Zonotrichia leucophrys
Family Emberizidae (Sparrows, Buntings)
Size: 7"
Season: Winter
Habitat: Brushy areas, woodland edges, gardens

The White-crowned Sparrow has a rounded head, sometimes with a raised peak, and a fairly long, slightly notched tail. It is brownish above, streaked on the mantle, and shows pale wing bars. The underside is grayish on the breast, fading to pale brown on the belly and flanks. The head is gray below the eyes and boldly patterned black and white above the eyes, with a white medial crown-stripe. The bill is bright yellow-orange. White-crowned Sparrows forage on the ground, often in loose flocks, scratching for insects, seeds, and berries. Their song is variable, but it usually starts with one longer whistle, followed by several faster notes. The adult is illustrated.

Song Sparrow,
Melospiza melodia
Family Emberizidae (Sparrows, Buntings)
Size: 6"
Season: Winter
Habitat: Thickets, shrubs, woodland edges near water

One of the most common sparrows, the Song Sparrow is fairly plump and has a long, rounded tail. It is brown and gray above with streaking, and white below with heavy dark or brownish streaking that often congeals into a discrete spot in the middle of the breast. The head has a dark crown with a gray medial stripe, dark eye-line, and dark malar stripe above the white chin. Song Sparrows are usually seen in small groups or individually, foraging on the ground for insects and seeds. The song is a series of chips and trills of variable pitch, and the call is a *chip-chip-chip*. The adult is illustrated.

TANAGERS, GROSBEAKS

Summer Tanager,
Piranga rubra
Family Cardinalidae (Tanagers, Grosbeaks)
Size: 7.75"
Season: Summer
Habitat: Mixed pine and oak woodlands

The Summer Tanager lives high in the tree canopy, where it voices a musical song and forages for insects and fruit. It is a relatively large, heavy-billed tanager with a crown that is often peaked in the middle. The male is variable shades of red over the entire body, while the female is olive or brownish-yellow above and dull yellow below. Juveniles are similar to the females but have a patchy red head and breast. The illustration shows an adult male.

Northern Cardinal,
Cardinalis cardinalis
Family Cardinalidae (Tanagers, Grosbeaks)
Size: 8.5"
Season: Year-round
Habitat: Woodlands with thickets,
suburban gardens

The Northern Cardinal with its thick, powerful bill eats mostly seeds but will also forage for fruit and insects. It is often found in pairs and is quite common at suburban feeders. It is a long-tailed songbird with a thick, short, orange bill and a tall crest. The male is red overall with a black mask and chin. The female is brownish above, dusky below, crested, with a dark front to the face. Juveniles are similar to the female but have a black bill. The voice is a musical *weeta-weeta* or *woit* heard from a tall, exposed perch. The illustration shows an adult male, below, and female, above.

Pyrrhuloxia, *Cardinalis sinuatus*
Family Cardinalidae (Tanagers, Grosbeaks)
Size: 8.75"
Season: Year-round
Habitat: Desert scrub; arid, open woodlands

The Pyrrhuloxia is built like the Northern Cardinal with a long tail, long, pointed crest, and a short, thick, yellow bill that is sharply curved. It is gray overall with patches of red on the tail, wings, crest, face, and in a stripe from the chin to the vent. The female is browner overall without red on the underparts and face. Pyrrhuloxias forage for insects and seeds. The voice is a series of a few, high, *wheet* notes, often sung while flicking the tail and erecting the crest. The adult male is illustrated.

Black-headed Grosbeak,

Pheucticus melanocephalus
Family Cardinalidae (Tanagers, Grosbeaks)
Size: 8.25"
Season: Summer in western Texas, transient migrant elsewhere
Habitat: Open woodlands, gardens, riparian areas

The Black-headed Grosbeak is a chunky, large-headed, short-tailed songbird with a massive, thick-based bill that enables it to eat very large seeds. The breeding male is black on the mantle, wings, and tail, with extensive white markings and streaks. The underparts, neck, and rump are rusty orange with whitish under-tail coverts. The head is black, and the bill is pale on the lower mandible and dark on the upper. The female is brownish above and pale tan below, with darker streaking. The head is brown, with a white supercilium and malar patch. Black-headed Grosbeaks eat insects, fruits, and seeds, and sometimes visit feeders. Their song consists of erratic, whistling warbles. The breeding female (top) and breeding male (bottom) are illustrated.

Blue Grosbeak,

Passerina caerulea
Family Cardinalidae (Tanagers, Grosbeaks)
Size: 6.5"
Season: Summer
Habitat: Woodland edges, thickets, fields

The name "grosbeak" derives from the French word *gros,* meaning large, and refers to the birds' massive, conical bills. The male Blue Grosbeak is azure blue overall with rufous wing bars and shoulder patches. It is black at the front of the face, and has a horn-colored bill. The female is brown overall and paler below, with lighter wing bars and lores. The similar Indigo Bunting is smaller in size and smaller-billed, and lacks the rufous color on the wings. Blue Grosbeaks eat seeds, fruit, and insects in open areas, and habitually flick their tails. They often perch and sing a meandering, warbling song for extended periods. The female (top) and male (bottom) are illustrated.

Indigo Bunting,

Passerina cyanea
Family Cardinalidae (Tanagers,
Grosbeaks)
Size: 5.5"
Season: Summer in eastern Texas,
transient migrant elsewhere
Habitat: Brush, open woodlands, fields

Often occurring in large flocks, the Indigo Bunting forages mostly on the ground for insects, berries, and seeds. It is a compact, small songbird with a short, thick bill. The male is entirely blue; the head is a dark, purplish-blue and the body is a lighter, sky blue. The female is brownish-gray above, duller below, with faint streaking on the breast meeting a white throat. The winter male is smudged with patchy gray, brown, and white. They perch in treetops voicing their undulating, chirping melodies. The illustration shows a breeding male, below, and female, above.

Painted Bunting, *Passerina ciris*

Family Cardinalidae (Tanagers,
Grosbeaks)
Size: 5.5"
Season: Summer
Habitat: Edges of woodlands, brushy
areas, gardens

Like a rainbow on wings, the Painted Bunting is one of our most colorful birds. It is similar in shape to other buntings and the plumage is markedly different between the sexes. The male has a green mantle and wings, red-orange to rusty underparts and rump, and a brilliant blue head with red eye-rings. The female is yellowish-green above and pale yellow-green below with pale eye-rings. Often secretive and difficult to find, Painted Buntings scamper in the low understory or on the ground for insects, seeds, and fruit. However, they may also visit feeders. The illustration shows an adult male, below, and female, above.

Eastern Meadowlark,

Sturnella magna
Family Icteridae (Blackbirds, Orioles, Grackles)
Size: 9.5"
Season: Year-round
Habitat: Open fields, grasslands, meadows

The Eastern Meadowlark is a chunky, short-tailed icterid with a flat head and a long, pointed bill. It is heavily streaked and barred above, and yellow beneath with dark streaking. The head has a dark crown, white superciliary stripe, dark eye-lines, and yellow chin. On the upper breast is a black V-shaped necklace that becomes quite pale during the winter months. Nonbreeding plumage is much paler overall. Meadowlarks gather in loose flocks to pick through the grass for insects and seeds. They often perch on telephone wires or posts to sing their short, whistling phrases. The breeding adult is illustrated.

Brown-headed Cowbird,

Molothrus ater
Family Icteridae (Blackbirds, Orioles, Grackles)
Size: 7.5"
Season: Year-round
Habitat: Woodland edges, pastures with livestock, grassy fields

The Brown-headed Cowbird is a stocky, short-winged, short-tailed blackbird with a short, conical bill. The male is glossy black overall, with a chocolate-brown head, but is sometimes much lighter in western populations. The female is light brown overall, with faint streaking on the underparts and a pale throat. Cowbirds often feed in flocks with other blackbirds, picking seeds and insects from the ground, and their voice is a number of gurgling, squeaking phrases. They practice brood parasitism, whereby they lay their eggs in the nests of other passerine species that then raise their young. Hence, their presence often reduces the populations of other songbirds. The dark adult male is illustrated.

Red-winged Blackbird,

Agelaius phoeniceus
Family Icteridae (Blackbirds, Orioles,
Grackles)
Size: 8.5"
Season: Year-round
Habitat: Marshes, meadows,
agricultural areas near water

The Red-winged Blackbird is a widespread, ubiquitous, chunky meadow-dweller that forms huge flocks during the nonbreeding season. The male is deep black overall, with bright orange-red lesser coverts and pale medial coverts that form an obvious shoulder patch in flight but may be partially concealed on the perched bird. The female is barred tan and dark brown overall, with a pale superciliary stripe and malar patch. Red-winged Blackbirds forage marshland for insects, spiders, and seeds. Their voice is a loud, raspy, vibrating *konk-a-leee* given from a perch atop a tall reed or branch. The female (top) and male (bottom) are illustrated.

Common Grackle, *Quiscalus quiscula*

Family Icteridae (Blackbirds, Orioles,
Grackles)
Size: 9"
Season: Year-round
Habitat: Meadows, pastures,
open woodlands, urban areas

The Common Grackle is a large blackbird but smaller than the Boat-tailed Grackle. The body is elongated with a long, heavy bill and long tail, which is fatter toward the tip and is often folded into a keel shape. Plumage is overall black with a metallic sheen of purple on the head and brown on the wings and underside. The eyes are a contrasting light yellow color. Quite social, Grackles form huge flocks with other blackbirds and forage on the ground for just about any kind of food, including insects, grains, refuse, and crustaceans. The voice is a high-pitched, rasping trill. The illustration shows an adult male.

Boat-tailed Grackle,

Quiscalus major
Family Icteridae (Blackbirds, Orioles, Grackles)
Size: 14-16", males larger than females
Season: Year-round along the Gulf Coast
Habitat: Meadows, pastures, open woodlands, urban areas

The Boat-tailed Grackle is larger than the Common Grackle and less likely to form large flocks. It has long legs and a long, broad, spatula-shaped tail that is often folded in a keel shape. The male is black overall, with a metallic, blue-green sheen over the head and body. The female is smaller with a shorter tail, is brownish overall, and has a lighter head with dark striping along the eye lines, under the crown, and along the malar area. The eyes of northern birds are light yellow, while those farther south have darker, brown eyes. Boat-tailed Grackles pick the ground for insects, seeds, and crustaceans. The adult male (bottom) and female (top) are illustrated.

Bullock's Oriole, *Icterus bullockii*

Family Icteridae (Blackbirds, Orioles, Grackles)
Size: 9"
Season: Summer
Habitat: Deciduous woodlands, suburban gardens, parks

The Bullock's Oriole is a flat-crowned and relatively short-tailed icterid with a pointed but broad-based bill. The male is black on the mantle and wings, with a large white patch on the wing coverts and white edges to the flight feathers. The body and rump are golden-orange, and the head is golden-orange with a black chin, eye-lines, and crown. The tail is orange, with a dark center and tips. Females are gray on the back, pale below, and yellow on the tail, head, and breast. Bullock's Orioles eat insects or berries in the tree canopy, and sing in a series of chatterings and *chips*. The Bullock's Oriole and Baltimore Oriole are sometimes considered one species, the Northern Oriole. The breeding female (top) and breeding male (bottom) are illustrated.

Orchard Oriole, *Icterus spurius*
Family Icteridae (Blackbirds, Orioles, Grackles)
Size: 7"
Season: Summer
Habitat: Deciduous woodlands, suburban gardens, parks

The Orchard Oriole is a small oriole with a relatively thin, short bill, and a short tail that it often tilts sideways. The male is black above with a red rump and a black, hooded head. The underside is reddish or orange-brown with a similarly colored shoulder patch. The lower mandible is light, blue-gray. Females are markedly different, being greenish-gray above and bright yellow below with two white wing bars. The juvenile is similar to the female but has a black chin and lores. Orchard Orioles feed in trees for insects, fruit, and nectar, and emit high, erratic, musical whistles and *chirps*. The illustration shows an adult male, below, and female, above.

House Finch,
Carpodacus mexicanus
Family Fringillidae (Finches)
Size: 6"
Season: Year-round
Habitat: Woodland edges, urban areas

The House Finch is a western species that has been introduced to eastern North America, and is now common and widespread across the country. It is a relatively slim finch with a longish, slightly notched tail and a short, conical bill with a downcurved culmen. The male is brown above, with streaking on the back, and pale below, with heavy streaking. An orange-red wash pervades the supercilium, throat, and upper breast. The female is a drab gray-brown, with similar streaking on the back and underside, and no red on the face or breast. House Finches have a variable diet that includes seeds, insects, and fruit, and they are often the most abundant birds at feeders. The House Finch's voice is a rapid, musical warble. The adult male is illustrated.

American Goldfinch, *Spinus tristis*
Family Fringillidae (Finches)
Size: 5"
Season: Winter
Habitat: Open fields, marshes, urban feeders

The American Goldfinch is a small, cheerful, social finch with a short, notched tail and a small, conical bill. In winter, it is brownish-gray, lighter underneath, with black wings and tail. There are two white wing bars, and bright yellow on the shoulders, around the eyes, and along the chin. In breeding plumage, the male becomes light yellow across the back, underside, and head; develops a black forehead and loreal area; and the bill becomes orange. Females look similar to the winter males. American Goldfinches forage by actively searching for insects and seeds of all kinds, particularly thistle seeds. The voice is a meandering, musical warble that includes high *cheep* notes. The breeding female (top) and breeding male (bottom) are illustrated.

House Sparrow, *Passer domesticus*
Family Passeridae (Old World Sparrows)
Size: 6.25"
Season: Year-round
Habitat: Urban environments, rural pastures

Introduced from Europe, the House Sparrow is ubiquitous in almost every city in the United States and is often the only sparrow-type bird seen in urban areas. It is stocky, aggressive, and gregarious, and has a relatively large head and a short, finch-like bill. Males are streaked brown and black above and are pale below. The lores, chin, and breast are black, while the crown and auriculars are gray. There are prominent white wing bars at the median coverts. In winter, the male lacks the dark breast patch. Females are drab overall, with a lighter bill and a pale supercilium. House Sparrows have a highly varied diet, including grains, insects, berries, and crumbs from the local cafe. The sparrow's voice is a series of rather unmusical *chirps*. The breeding female (top) and breeding male (bottom) are illustrated.

Index

About the Author/Illustrator

Todd Telander is a naturalist/illustrator/artist living in Walla Walla, Washington. He has studied and illustrated wildlife since 1989, while living in California, Colorado, New Mexico, and Washington. He graduated from the University of California at Santa Cruz with degrees in biology, environmental studies, and scientific illustration and has since illustrated numerous books and other publications, including  FalconGuides' Scats and Tracks series. His wife, Kirsten Telander, is a writer and teacher, and he has two sons, Miles and Oliver. His work can be viewed online at www.toddtelander.com.